BARKER PLAYS TEN

Howard Barker

PLAYS TEN

ANHO
EXQUISITE
IRRESPECTIVE
DISTANCE
IMMENSE KISS
CRITIQUE OF PURE FEELING

OBERON BOOKS
LONDON

WWW.OBERONBOOKS.COM

This collection first published in 2018 by Oberon Books Ltd
521 Caledonian Road, London N7 9RH
Tel: +44 (0) 20 7607 3637 / Fax: +44 (0) 20 7607 3629
e-mail: info@oberonbooks.com
www.oberonbooks.com

A catalogue record for this book is available from the British
Library.

PB ISBN: 9781786824219
E ISBN: 9781786824226

Cover photography by Eduardo Houth.

eBook conversion by Lapiz Digital Services, India.

Visit www.oberonbooks.com to read more about all our books
and to buy them. You will also find features, author interviews and
news of any author events, and you can sign up for e-newsletters
so that you're always first to hear about our new releases.

Contents

AHNO

Characters

AHNO	A Prince of Now
APRON	His Mother
FALLA	His Lover
IRASH	His Servant
A MURDERER	Of 8 Children
STRAPP	A General Practitioner
PRITTY	A Commissar of Ahno
ECZEMAS	A Former Teacher of Ahno
BURNOW	A Novice
CASTOR	" "
LIEVENS	" "
QUARTZ	A Girl Off Remand
JUTLAND	A Clever Child
ATTENDANT	
GUARD	
UNDERTAKER	
A HOUND	

A single chair, unoccupied.

APRON: Lay a finger on that boy I'll blind you / lay a finger /
lay a finger / lay a finger on that boy /

(She laughs, shaking her head.)

I'll blind you /

(A man enters, grey and distinguished.)

lay a /

(Her laughter consumes her.)

lay a /

(The man sits.)

finger on that boy I'll /

(She chokes. Her shoulders shake.)

blind you /

(She recovers.)

AHNO: You were the best /

APRON: Was I /

AHNO: The best /

APRON: Was I /

AHNO: I didn't know it at the time /

APRON: At the time /

AHNO: At the time I didn't /

APRON: At the time /

(She smiles wanly.)

at the time /

AHNO: It isn't possible /

APRON: No /

AHNO: To know things at the time /

APRON: *(Suddenly.)* Lay a finger on that boy /

AHNO: And if it were /

APRON: Lay a finger /

AHNO: If it were possible /

APRON: Lay a finger on that boy /

AHNO: It's not obvious to me /

APRON: *(Coolly.)* I'll blind you /

AHNO: It would be /

    (He lacks the word, briefly.)

    beneficial /

    (They are silent for a time.)

    I dislike the beneficial /

    (And waits.)

    bene /

    bene /

    (His smile is pained.)

    bene-everything I hate /

    (A woman marches in. She stops. She seems resolute.)

FALLA: My husband has to know /

    (AHNO regards her dispassionately.)

    I say know / how could he know /

    (She bites her lip in her anxiety.)

    not know / not know / of course he cannot <u>know</u> /

(She looks boldly at AHNO.)

he can however / be informed /

(AHNO'S gaze is unaltered. He does not assist her.)

for forty years we have / my husband and I /

AHNO: Forty-seven /

(FALLA is rebuked and resents it.)

FALLA: For forty-seven years we have /

(She stops.)

I so dislike you / so / so / so dislike you /

(And proceeds.)

lived in perfect amity / telling and hearing / hearing and forgiving / his tolerance / his generosity /

(She stops abruptly.)

I saw your fingers move /

(Her lips go tight.)

impatience made your fingers move /

AHNO: *(In his own time.)* Inform him /

(FALLA collects herself, lowers her head once and gathers up her skirts as if to leave.)

your appetite for cruelty is no more sordid than his pleasure in enduring it /

(She stares witheringly. He does not flinch.)

I daresay /

(She cannot move. He cannot cease.)

and he must be thinking / 'she's 74 / the era of forgiving has drawn to a close / no more sobbing in the mirthless corridors of the great house / it's birds' eggs now / birds' eggs and opera scores' /

(He throws back his head and laughs. The laugh is genuine.)

go and inform /

(They stare.)

watch him go down like a stricken ship / and then return / return and strip for me / pristine your garments / a froth from which you step perfect /

(He is visibly moved in his passion.)

perfect in decay /

(She reciprocates his longing.)

FALLA: I /

(She aches.)

I can't move /

(She creates a laugh.)

I can't / I can't /

(She cries out.)

I belong here /

AHNO: Yes /

FALLA: *(A passionate affirmation.)* I do / I do / I belong here /

(She sobs, half-rage, half-joy. APRON intervenes to conclude things.)

APRON: Lay a finger on that boy /

FALLA: Darling /

APRON: Lay a finger /

FALLA: I'm wrecked / I'm wrecked / say you're wrecked too /

APRON: Lay a finger on that boy /

(AHNO does not satisfy her. She emits a massive sob that seems to dislocate her body.)

I'll blind you /

(FALLA slowly draws herself up. AHNO watches her, frowning yet detached.)

FALLA: You're not / are you /

(She sniffs, she tilts up her chin with contempt.)

you're not wrecked? /

(AHNO replies to APRON, not to FALLA.)

AHNO: He did not however / did he? / the man who was my father? /

(FALLA turns and with a contrived dignity, departs.)

lay a finger on me? /

APRON: *(Nostalgic.)* He did not / no /

AHNO: The thought of you / in dead of night / plunging some kitchen knife / one / two / was adequate / I daresay / given you /

(He studies APRON.)

were wild /

(They smile. AHNO looks after FALLA.)

I don't want that woman /

APRON: No /

AHNO: She is a liar /

APRON: Yes /

(APRON shrugs.)

yes /

(And shrugs again.)

a liar / anyone can see / and this dishonesty /

(She shrugs yet again.)

were you to strip her naked /

(She pulls a face.)

would induce a /

(She enjoys the phrase she invents.)

crisis of impotence in you /

(AHNO turns his face slowly to her.)

wouldn't it? /

(They look. They explode in laughter. AHNO is impelled to stand and stride about, then stopping suddenly, to look at her. He bursts out laughing again.)

AHNO: You did / you <u>did</u> blind him /

(His laughter rolls on.)

APRON: I would have / I would have / Ahno / blinded anyone who /

AHNO: *(A refrain.)* <u>Laid</u> <u>a</u> <u>finger</u> /

APRON: On <u>you</u> / <u>yes</u> /

(Their mutual pleasure subsides.)

AHNO: She is a liar / and the husband / so is he /

(He is mild, considered.)

in the field of matrimony / and only there / lying does not irk me /

(He lifts his gaze to APRON.)

the moral platitudes I brought home from school my mother cleansed me of / as if she plucked lice out my hair with tweezers /

APRON: *(Deeply.)* I saved you /

AHNO: *(His regard equally deep.)* Arguably / arguably /

(*A servant strides through.*)

IRASH: Somebody /

(*He brusquely indicates.*)

APRON: Don't say somebody / say who /

IRASH: *(Departing.)* A murderer /

AHNO: Tell the murderer to wait /

(*IRASH stops. A second of irritation passes over him. He turns and retraces his steps.*)

APRON: And bow /

(*IRASH looks at APRON with a cruel resentment.*)

do you know who this is? /

IRASH: I do /

APRON: Bow then /

(*IRASH allows time to pass before bowing his head to AHNO. He then goes to retreat to the door.*)

AHNO: That won't do /

(*IRASH stops. His mouth tight.*)

repeat the bow but this time bow because you want to /

(*IRASH is seething. He struggles with himself. A murderer slouches in. AHNO senses rather than sees him.*)

not you /

(*The MURDERER stops.*)

not you / not you /

(*The MURDERER sullenly withdraws. IRASH is struggling.*)

now bow / bow because I'm worthy of your bowing /

(IRASH is stiff with his pain.)

be beautiful /

(And still seethes.)

oh / be beautiful /

(He waits, and IRASH concedes the bow. He withdraws after the murderer. APRON studies her son with love. AHNO is deep in thought.)

what did I mean when I said / 'I do not want that woman?' /

(APRON gazes blankly at her son.)

she's ill / and every day weighs less /

(He ponders.)

that is not the reason /

(And ponders.)

ill / but still so / her walk so / and her small head poised on her neck so /

(He frowns.)

it must give her agony /

(And struggles to identify.)

no / her sickness is not /

(He casts a look to APRON, almost a plea.)

I like her sickness /

(APRON is patient. AHNO seems to suffer, and to resolve it, stands up abruptly and calls.)

come in / come in /

(He strides about. He looks to his mother.)

go now / go now /

(APRON goes to kiss him, but he flicks a hand at her. She obeys and goes to leave, then stops, a look of dread on her face.)

APRON: Are you /

(He casts a glance at her.)

is he /

(By way of reply AHNO shows a small pistol and replaces it. APRON is satisfied and goes out as the MURDERER slouches in.)

AHNO: Have a seat /

(He walks in his normal impatient way.)

take the seat you vile and ugly murderer / take the seat /

(The MURDERER seems bemused and refrains from the invitation.)

you don't want the seat / or you do want the seat but think you are not vile / not vile nor ugly / you are both /

(He stops, gazing at the murderer.)

five girls you killed / you smile / you think / <u>five</u> / <u>five</u> / you laugh at <u>five</u> / laugh / laugh /

(The MURDERER declines this invitation also. IRASH enters and this time bows.)

IRASH: She's here /

AHNO: I'm occupied /

IRASH: I said / I said he's occupied /

(IRASH attends. Suddenly the MURDERER laughs. AHNO points a finger at him.)

AHNO: That's good / that is the laugh /

(The MURDERER now goes to the chair and sits. AHNO pretends to be amicable.)

she can't sleep / all night she thinks of me / and at 75 / you need sleep /

(This revelation makes the MURDERER uncomfortable. His smile is awkward.)

oh yes / and pecks at food / you know how it is with love / no appetite /

(They look at one another, but it is AHNO who outstares the murderer in the long silence.)

IRASH: I'll tell her /

AHNO: Tell her again / say <u>very</u> / say <u>very</u> occupied /

(IRASH bows, and departs. AHNO is casual.)

I'm hanging you myself /

(The murderer looks aghast.)

to be precise / I'm pulling the lever / the knot / the rope / etcetera / that's not my /

(He shrugs.)

I'd make a mess of it /

(The word he has uttered gives him pause for thought.)

<u>a</u> <u>mess</u> <u>of</u> <u>death</u> / the sort of mess familiar to you /

(His gaze on the murderer is maddened but still. He sustains it for a long time.)

I know everything / everything you did /

(The murderer is afraid of AHNO.)

laugh /

(He disdains to.)

<u>laugh</u> /

(The murderer invents a slow laugh.)

it's funny / funny because no other knows / but me and you / and soon / it won't be known even to you /

(He gazes and gazes.)

surely that's proper? /

(Time passes. The murderer utters at last.)

MURDERER: Prick /

(The word is a weapon without an edge. AHNO merely looks. He recovers his levity.)

AHNO: I'll tell you why / in this instance / the executioner must be me / after all / I am who I am / and need do nothing unless it pleases me to /

(The murderer heeds.)

they said / these scarce and demi / friends of mine / if you like death so much / shouldn't you do the thing yourself / thinking me so fragile / so fastidious / and so loving beauty / I'd never /

(He seems uncritical of the murderer now.)

but it is beautiful / to be the killer of a man like you / and the only pity's this /

(He weighs the words.)

you can't be killed five times /

(The murderer grins back.)

MURDERER: Eight /

AHNO: Eight /

(AHNO disguises the depths of his loathing in a smile that almost seems a tribute. The murderer endows his word with deeper contempt still.)

MURDERER: Prick /

(Without haste, AHNO removes the pistol from his pocket and fires it into the foot of the murderer, who screams in pain, staggers and

11

pulls the chair on top of himself. AHNO seems frustrated with himself as the servant hurries in, followed by APRON. He replaces the gun.)

AHNO: *(to IRASH.)* I'll see her now /

(Satisfied her son is safe, APRON discreetly withdraws.)

now / say /

(AHNO recovers.)

now / now /

(IRASH goes to hurry out.)

<u>bow</u> /

(IRASH stops in his tracks.)

you did not bow /

(As the murderer sobs and howls, IRASH, delighted with his master, bows without sarcasm and goes out. An officer enters and without orders, clips his handcuffs on the murderer and thrusts him away. AHNO stands the fallen chair on its legs. FALLA, pale with apprehension, enters. She gazes at AHNO, who is not yet restored, and adjusts his cuffs unnecessarily. At last he is ready to look at her.)

FALLA: *(A surge of relief.)* I've told him /

(She inhales desperately.)

<u>I've</u> <u>told</u> <u>him</u> /

(AHNO is objective.)

oh / the poor dear man /

(She lurches into the chair. AHNO declines to comfort her.)

his face fell / as if a cliff / undermined by the gnawing of the waves / gave up the struggle to stay vertical / and collapsed / so slowly and so silently collapsed /

(She bites her lip.)

with relief / perhaps /

(She waits for a response that does not come.)

he wants to speak with you /

(A slight revulsion is discernible in AHNO.)

darling /

(A silence descends on them. They are dead still and stare, one behind the other, FALLA seated, AHNO standing directly behind her. A dog barks, ceases, barks again.)

AHNO: *(Calling.)* Is that my dog? /

(There is no response. In the silence, the bark comes again, identically.)

is that my dog? /

(IRASH hurries in. He frowns.)

IRASH: You don't have a dog /

(All three are motionless. At last, AHNO is animated.)

do you /

(AHNO observes his servant.)

have a dog? /

(AHNO cannot reply. A plump, undistinguished man appears and attends on them. FALLA, emerging, turns to him.)

FALLA: Darling /

(She frowns at her husband. She stands and going to him, wipes his lip with a handkerchief. He does not resist. FALLA is energetic suddenly.)

FALLA: I'll leave you two /

AHNO: No /

(She hesitates, surprised.)

FALLA: The two of you together /

AHNO: No /

(FALLA did not predict this. IRASH is equally uncertain of the situation. He bows and goes to edge away.)

for a moment I thought I had a dog /

(IRASH nods, as if he grasped this.)

a thoroughbred /

(IRASH nods again.)

highly strung /

(IRASH waits. AHNO reaches into his pocket.)

take this / take this in case /

(He extends the gun to IRASH, who accepts it, and goes to leave.)

in case / in case /

(IRASH understands. He looks at the stranger.)

IRASH: I was a lout /

(The stranger looks at the floor, as he has since he entered.)

he said / 'you need not be a lout' / I said / 'I like it' /

(He laughs, sniffing.)

he said / 'be a lout then / but be a lout for me' /

(He laughs and sniffs again. He judges the form of the stranger.)

you're a boxer /

(The stranger does not dissent.)

lay a finger on him I'll /

(IRASH bows to AHNO and goes out.)

lay a finger /

(IRASH has gone. In the following silence, FALLA plays with her fingers. AHNO waits. At last the stranger looks at AHNO.)

STRAPP: Look after her /

(AHNO gazes at STRAPP with contempt. Time passes.)

AHNO: Of course I shan't and you are fraudulent / the pair of you /

(He shifts his gaze to FALLA.)

but whereas I frequently experience the desire to kiss your wife between her legs /

(He allows the words to penetrate STRAPP.)

a desire so overwhelming it abolishes all criteria of lies / truth / or obligation /

(The married couple are still.)

no such servitude characterizes my relationship with you /

STRAPP: Silly /

AHNO: I have no relationship with you /

STRAPP: Mr Ahno /

AHNO: Though you may well flatter yourself you have acquired the status of a /

(He falters.)

a / participant in our intimacy / by virtue of the fact your wife /

(He is less vehement.)

appears to wish to include you in /

(He shrugs. He hesitates.)

our /

(He looks at STRAPP'S hands, hanging at his sides.)

yes / my servant is perceptive / your hands are boxer's hands / whereas you are a surgeon / I believe /

(STRAPP does not reply, but goes to the chair and takes it.)

you should have hit me / many months ago /

(He looks at FALLA.)

a single blow would have caused me to desist /

(He smiles.)

or even a raised fist /

STRAPP: Great is your love for my wife / Mr Ahno /

AHNO: Yes / but not greater than my love of my own face /

FALLA: *(At the limits.)* Do stop / do stop / do stop this / this /

(STRAPP aches for his wife. AHNO looks without emotion at her.)

this /

(She shakes her head pitifully. She ceases. Her head hangs.)

STRAPP: I'll go /

(He stands. He is forlorn.)

I came only to /

FALLA: *(A wail.)* Don't go /

(AHNO looks from husband to wife and back again. Time descends on them, a suffocating weight.)

AHNO: I do not want your wife / Mr /

(He frowns.)

ha /

(He shakes his head briefly.)

your name has slipped my memory /

(AHNO is puzzled by the fact.)

STRAPP: You forget my name / whereas I have no difficulty in remembering yours /

(AHNO observes him closely.)

the sight of us / like broken beggars in your hall /

FALLA: What do you mean you don't want me /

STRAPP: Fills you with shame / perhaps /

FALLA: What do you mean /

(She glares at AHNO.)

what do you mean /

(In her agony FALLA turns to her husband.)

what <u>does</u> <u>he</u> <u>mean</u> <u>he</u> <u>doesn't</u> <u>want</u> <u>me</u> /

(Her shrill cry imposes silence. STRAPP opens his mouth to speak comfort but closes it again. FALLA is in confusion.)

I am 74 years old / 74 and /

(She twists her head.)

74 and /

(She turns on AHNO.)

I hate you / hate you and /

(She shrinks.)

the things he says / when we are naked / the things he says /

(She draws herself up.)

I am not leaving here /

(She looks fiercely at AHNO.)

you bought me with those words / those words made me your possession / and I can't be unpossessed /

(She sustains her stare until she feels on the edge of collapse. She hurtles to the chair. She recovers sufficiently to look at her husband. A strange laugh issues from her.)

I came home / didn't I / wet from his body / wet from his words /

(STRAPP cannot meet his wife's eyes.)

and you were moved / so moved / and asked / politely / if I would let your hand beneath my clothes / the clothes I had dragged up / and flung on / minutes before / so your fingers could explore the lake my perished vulva had become /

(STRAPP is still. FALLA looks to AHNO.)

74 /

(She stands, restored.)

I'd like my own room /

(AHNO, without reflection, whistles for IRASH.)

it's years since I slept with a man /

(She is coy.)

it's not the sleeping / it's the waking up /

(IRASH appears and bows.)

AHNO: Show /

(He stops on the word.)

show my /

(And stops again.)

show <u>the doctor's wife</u> / the many rooms east of the library /

(IRASH is briefly puzzled.)

IRASH: <u>East</u> of the /

AHNO: <u>East of the library</u> / yes / and let her choose the one she / or the several / I don't mind /

(IRASH bows, and with his best effort, ushers FALLA. Her emotional crisis is best served by action, she well knows. With one look to STRAPP, she turns and goes. STRAPP stares at the floor.)

STRAPP: She takes medication for /

AHNO: I do not need to know that she takes medication for /

(STRAPP is silenced.)

continue / please / to be her physician / and charge the fees to me /

(STRAPP tilts his head in accord. He goes to depart but stops. His tone is bemused.)

STRAPP: It's years since I saw her naked /

(He smiles oddly.)

or without make-up / for that matter /

AHNO: *(Mildly.)* A fact which scarcely diminished your affection for her / I daresay /

(STRAPP is grateful for this perception and confesses more.)

STRAPP: I felt sure I'd /

(He shakes his head.)

<u>sure</u> / <u>sure</u> /

(And shakes it again.)

stupid to be <u>sure</u> /

(He sniffs.)

I'd bury her / or she'd bury me /

(He is forlorn, drained.)

AHNO: Go to your empty home now / polish the knocker on the door which / I observe / has been neglected recently / and in the perfect silence / which is a gift / a gift you might one day acknowledge / study your birds' eggs / read your opera scores /

(AHNO suddenly flings away his posture of civility.)

I <u>do</u> <u>not</u> <u>want</u> <u>your</u> <u>wife</u> / <u>God</u> <u>knows</u> /

(STRAPP is both awed and offended. He gawps.)

STRAPP: Then why /

AHNO: *(Thrusting the words back.)* <u>Then</u> <u>why</u> / <u>then</u> <u>why</u> /

(He glares at STRAPP.)

<u>then</u> <u>why</u> /

(STRAPP is apprehensive, and tentative.)

STRAPP: Return her to me /

(AHNO seems depleted.)

do the things you / what you / what she /

(He shrugs miserably.)

all things naked that you do / and half-naked / and scarcely-naked / and not naked at all / do it all / and at the end of it /

AHNO: *(Definitively.)* She will never be returned to you /

(STRAPP is persuaded. His head hangs. AHNO could grieve with him but prefers to deepen his own pain by contemplating it.)

is it so hard for you / a doctor / who perches on the rim of death / and stirs death with his fingers / to understand /

(He is perfect in articulation.)

<u>not-wanting</u> /

(STRAPP barely shrugs.)

are you so wrecked by pleasure / has pleasure so subordinated you / you cannot imagine even / what is beautiful in /

(The same dog barks.)

that is my dog /

(He listens for a moment.)

he says / my servant / it is not my dog / I have no dog / he says /

(He laughs briefly.)

still /

(It barks again.)

that's him /

(The dog puts an end to AHNO'S speculation. STRAPP knows this and goes to leave.)

your wife /

(STRAPP stops.)

naked as you say /

(He is desperate in his truth.)

I could faint /

(STRAPP is moved by his enemy. He makes a small move of his head and goes out. The dog barks on, and AHNO heeds it, as if it were fine music. A young man enters, his garments soiled, half-military. He is about to speak but AHNO stops him with a finger. Now IRASH marches in bearing an overcoat for AHNO.)

the thoroughbred /

(IRASH stops.)

fetch it /

(IRASH is puzzled. He looks briefly at the young man who ignores him. IRASH extends the coat for AHNO.)

IRASH: You're late /

AHNO: *(Extending his arms.)* It's a hound /

IRASH: *(Adjusting the coat.)* A hound / yes /

AHNO: You know a hound / do you /

IRASH: I think so / yes /

AHNO: A hound / and not a terrier /

IRASH: Not a terrier /

PRITTY: Long legs /

IRASH: I'll see what I can do /

(He senses AHNO'S frustration and stops plucking the coat.)

it's /

(He pulls a face.)

people are /

(He is reluctant.)

they love their dogs /

(His face is a spectacle of pain. AHNO and PRITTY watch. The bark comes again.)

AHNO: Weigh them down with money / more and more money / until it snaps the little branch of loyalty you have described /

(IRASH is relieved by this. He bows.)

IRASH: You're late /

AHNO: I <u>am</u> late /

(He goes to leave.)

did Mrs Strapp find any room that satisfied her? /

IRASH: She did / but /

AHNO: Which? /

IRASH: Several / she wanted one that got the morning light /

AHNO: All those which overlook the garden receive full light /

IRASH: *(Exploding.)* <u>You're</u> <u>late</u> /

   (AHNO stares at IRASH, incredulous at his insolence.)

a man is waiting to die / in a /

   (He squirms.)

in a horrible place / and you /

   (AHNO refutes his servant by simply going to the chair and sitting. He crosses his legs. IRASH goes on.)

talk about dogs /

   (He shakes his head.)

dogs and some old woman who /

   (He knows he is doomed and lets out a cry.)

likes light /

   (He sobs. AHNO is not disposed to be cruel.)

AHNO: The old woman is my darling /

IRASH: Yes /

AHNO: And I must have the dog /

   (IRASH nods fervently. AHNO is deliberately slow to proceed, while IRASH fidgets impatiently.)

the vile individual you have such pity for /

   (He watches IRASH.)

23

of all depravity that you might add to murder / that he did /

(IRASH nods. AHNO delays.)

play chess / shall we? /

(IRASH squirms.)

play chess? /

(IRASH is silent. In his own time, AHNO rises to his feet. He and PRITTY go out. The dog barks. IRASH, without enthusiasm, is about to set off in search of it when APRON enters. IRASH barely acknowledges her, but she stops him with two words.)

APRON: Ahno's God /

(IRASH stops. He smiles superciliously.)

IRASH: Ahno's mum says Ahno's God /

(He sniffs.)

Ahno believes her /

(He turns to face APRON.)

is that conclusive / I don't know /

(APRON looks without rancour. IRASH is uncomfortable.)

he's gone to kill a killer / so /

(He shrugs.)

God / ish /

(And again.)

God / ish / surely? /

(He is suddenly afraid of APRON.)

I like Mr Ahno / he has been good to me / and if he's God /

(He is without guile.)

good /

(He bites his lip.)

now I must do God's will / that dog / he / if it is a <u>he</u> / has heard God wants him / and /

(He falters. He looks directly at APRON.)

Mr Ahno / did he have a dad? /

(APRON is adamant.)

APRON: What do you think /

IRASH: *(Tentatively.)* God's dad / I /

(He squirms.)

I was a choirboy / scripture we did ten minutes of / and /

(He dares.)

if I remember properly / God <u>is</u> the father / and /

(APRON watches.)

God the father can't be fathered /

(Her gaze weakens him.)

can't because /

APRON: *(At last.)* He was fathered /

(IRASH nods fervently. He is suddenly overcome by a wave of laughter which subverts his contrived good manners. APRON watches. IRASH reels, unable to speak coherently.)

IRASH: Dog / I / get the /

(He chokes.)

got to get the /

(He surrenders to the laugh, but manages to utter through it.)

it's not funny /

(As he shakes his head to clear it, PRITTY enters. His appearance checks IRASH'S nerves.)

PRITTY: He's walking /

(APRON and IRASH nod.)

kicking up the leaves / gazing at the sky / and singing one of the four songs he says <u>are</u> songs / the rest / he says / are lies /

APRON: I sang them /

PRITTY: His mother sang them / how could he know them otherwise? /

(He is respectful.)

Ahno knows so little / of what the world knows / don't you find? /

(They say nothing.)

when I first met Ahno / he said / 'my mind's a fortress / and behind the walls /

(PRITTY smiles.)

<u>items</u> /

(He muses.)

<u>few</u> / but precious / <u>items</u>' /

(He frowns.)

'such as?' / I said /

(And laughs.)

'if I revealed the items / I should not need the walls' /

(He looks at APRON.)

your son replied /

(He does not glance at IRASH.)

no luck with the dog / then / I heard it whine / I thought / he's failed /

(Now he turns to IRASH, who goes to leave but encounters AHNO, returning. AHNO seems thoughtful but not anguished. IRASH bows, humiliated.)

IRASH: Fetching the dog / I /

(He edges out.)

fetching it /

(And is gone. APRON goes to her son and kisses his cheek. PRITTY idly walks downstage.)

PRITTY: These wives /

(He frowns.)

these / am I sentimental / these <u>unmarried</u> wives /

(AHNO goes to the chair and sits.)

you'd think / hearing the shots / they'd scream / 'my loved one' / 'my / my /

(He ponders.)

oh my' /

(He shrugs.)

something /

(He shrugs again.)

or clasp us round our knees / crying /

(AHNO mildly laughs, his gaze on the floor.)

I don't know /

(He shakes his head.)

<u>something</u> /

(He hesitates, a memory absorbing him.)

I said <u>upstairs</u> / for some reason I wanted to be undressed / undressed / and on a bed / am I sentimental / she looked at me / an unnatural smile /

AHNO: Not to be wondered at /

PRITTY: Not to be wondered at / the unnatural smiles of these unmarried wives / and I <u>am</u> /

AHNO: You are /

PRITTY: So sentimental / I think if I met one / one woman / in one village / who said /

(He seems at a loss.)

'I'd rather die than' /

(He shakes his head, he resumes.)

'you're narrow-chested' / she says / half-admiring / or half-critical / you can't be sure / it's talk for talk's sake / and calls me darling / <u>darling</u> / with her husband lying on the floor /

AHNO: You're so / so /

PRITTY: Sentimental / yes / I am / and better / better than a whore / <u>extends</u> <u>herself</u> /

(He stops.)

I never go to whores /

(He laughs.)

I don't know how a whore /

(He likes this phrase.)

<u>extends</u> <u>herself</u> /

(He laughs, in a faintly melancholy way.)

and all these photographs / in frames / weddings / ponies / holidays /

(He turns to AHNO for the first time.)

they grin / always they grin / and the grinning is the same /

(He is injured by everything he describes. He proceeds.)

she kisses me /

(He reflects.)

<u>kisses</u> / and <u>kisses</u> /

(He winces at the memory.)

I think / these unmarried wives / why don't they turn their heads away? /

(AHNO heeds PRITTY, who ceases to wonder when AHNO changes the subject.)

AHNO: My dread was this / he'd make a scene /

PRITTY: You said /

AHNO: The ethical and intellectual aspects of the execution / both of which dictated my decision to be there / were swept aside by this profound anxiety / shared by everyone so far as I could see / that he'd /

(He meditates briefly.)

howl / swear / fling /

(He ponders.)

and make it sordid /

(He frowns.)

I was obliged to recognize how much I cared / not for <u>him</u> / who / like some dying king / was privileged to be the subject of an extraordinary ritual / but for the act that would destroy him /

(He aches to define things.)

As I leaned on the lever I required to know he rendered me / and through me / the world / the homage owed to beauty /

(He pursues the thought relentlessly.)

he had defiled beauty / God knows he had / but beauty insisted on itself / and if he slammed one door on beauty / it walked back through another / in the form of retribution /

(He nods. He is satisfied to have articulated things.)

dimly he knew this / whilst / in the way of all poor minds / extracting humour from his situation /

(He is almost affectionate.)

'I have a raging tooth' / he said / 'so it was either you / or the dentist / and I hate dentists' /

(He frowns.)

I smiled / why did I / I should not have done /

(AHNO is pained.)

he might have thought / in that semi-second left to him before I flung the lever /

(He shrugs.)

'we share something / in this the lord and I are one' /

(He looks at PRITTY.)

I preferred it when he called me prick /

(And smiles at him.)

I am not sentimental /

(PRITTY acknowledges this with a smile.)

whilst knowing everything that might make me so /

(PRITTY looks on AHNO with devotion.)

I am thin-skinned /

APRON: *(Inspired.)* Lay a finger on that boy /

AHNO: Oh / so thin my skin /

APRON: I'll blind you /

(Neither PRITTY nor AHNO reacts to APRON. A strange intimacy flows between all three before the distant barking of the dog breaks the charm of the moment. PRITTY goes to leave, activated.)

AHNO: I'll come /

(PRITTY stops.)

on one of these tours that you do / and see the windmills / and the oxen ploughing / and the /

(PRITTY acknowledges AHNO'S humour.)

the millpond / and / and /

PRITTY: The five cars in the driveway /

AHNO: The shepherds chewing straws / the / the /

PRITTY: Hundred foot long swimming pools /

(AHNO ceases his listing. He smiles at PRITTY.)

we would be so honoured by your presence / and for them /

(His smile is ambiguous.)

the rock stars and the businessmen / to see your face /

(He shakes his head in wonder.)

AHNO: I may not leave the car /

PRITTY: No / but /

(He contemplates it.)

this dim profile behind the glass /

(He need not continue. AHNO tilts his head, an instruction for PRITTY to withdraw. He does so. For a moment, AHNO and his mother are silent.)

APRON: You must not <u>do</u> /

(He hears without replying.)

you know that /

AHNO: Shh /

APRON: That you must not <u>do</u> /

(She will not risk irritating her son, and goes to leave, but cannot.)

the hanging /

(She persists.)

that's adequate / adequate to show you /

AHNO: Shh /

APRON: <u>Can</u> / should you want to / <u>do</u> /

(AHNO waits.)

but <u>don't</u> /

(AHNO understands her point. He is stiffly patient.)

AHNO: Yes /

(Still she hangs back.)

APRON: <u>Doing</u> / it's like /

AHNO: Yes /

(She is reluctant but must persist.)

APRON: That woman /

(Now he just looks at her.)

you start / you think / 'that's adequate' /

(She is determined to finish her admonition.)

it isn't / it isn't adequate / you keep going back /

(They exchange a long regard.)

AHNO: Yes /

(She might go now, but still holds back.)

APRON: <u>Thinking</u> /

(Now he nods.)

is what <u>you</u> do /

(AHNO folds his hands. His ill-temper dissipates. They look at one another with the strain and beauty of their history, neither resolved. She departs as FALLA enters, looking at APRON as she goes.)

AHNO: I'm a slave / she says / a slave to you / did you find a room / a suitable room / it's true / I am / and sometimes howl against my slavery / but not for long /

(He looks at her.)

not <u>howl</u> /

(And is ravished by her.)

<u>mutter</u> /

(He meditates.)

as all slaves do / and it's as well I merely mutter / anything more vehement and I might damage you /

(He looks.)

you're thinner / thinner since noon /

(She does not confirm or deny this.)

when you are dead / I'll wash and bury you myself / that's understood / we are agreed /

FALLA: Yes /

AHNO: And when I say bury / I mean dig / the six feet necessary /

FALLA: Three is adequate /

AHNO: *(Charmed.)* Three / only three /

FALLA: No vixen will uncover me /

AHNO: Why should she /

FALLA: Fuck now /

AHNO: For your desiccated and /

FALLA: Fuck / darling /

AHNO: Unappetizing parts? /

(They watch, adoring.)

'don't feed that shrivelled bitch to us' / the cubs complain /

FALLA: Kiss / then /

AHNO: Used to the fatty hearts of lawyers /

FALLA: Kiss /

AHNO: And pop star brain /

(His gaze alters her. She turns in her agony.)

FALLA: I do not / I simply do not know myself /

(She covers her face with her hands.)

and if I'm sick / you are the sickness /

(She turns to him, pitiful and resentful.)

I wanted to spend my last years doing /

(She does not know.)

nothing /

(But asserts it.)

beautiful / beautiful / <u>nothing</u> /

(She is briefly forlorn, then urgent.)

I must lie down / my hips / my /

(She panics.)

knees / I'm /

AHNO: Lie down / I'll come to you /

FALLA: *(Shrieking.)* <u>I</u> <u>don't</u> <u>want</u> <u>you</u> <u>to</u> <u>come</u> <u>to</u> <u>me</u> /

(She glares.)

<u>come</u> <u>to</u> <u>me</u> /

(More fiercely still.)

what does that mean / <u>come</u> <u>to</u> <u>me</u> / I know what <u>come</u> <u>to</u> <u>me</u> means /

(AHNO is placid, apparently.)

<u>come</u> <u>to</u> <u>me</u> /

(She seethes. Her breath is hard. She alters catastrophically.)

come to me / then / I wish I'd never met you / come to me
/

(She drifts away, unsteady on her feet. AHNO looks to the ceiling, as if biding his time. After a few seconds, FALLA returns, her footsteps stronger.)

I'm leaving /

(He slowly observes her.)

this is /

(She shakes her head.)

<u>not</u> /

(And shakes it more.)

not /

(She is speechless now. Her thin hand rises and falls.)

simply not /

(She writhes.)

simply not and I'm leaving /

(She turns and goes back to her room, exactly as IRASH enters, frowning.)

IRASH: This dog /

AHNO: My dog /

IRASH: Your dog /

AHNO: My hound /

IRASH: Your hound / yes / I go to /

AHNO: *(Cutting him off.)* She's not to leave /

   (IRASH is puzzled.)

   the old woman / the fragile and cantankerous old woman with whom I am in love /

   (IRASH looks uncomfortable.)

   is not to leave /

   (IRASH is reluctant.)

   lock her in her room if necessary / you have the keys /

IRASH: I have the keys /

AHNO: Try not to handle her / she bruises easily / but she won't fight / and she won't scream / she treats her body as if it were a relic / which it is / the relic of her own arrogance /

IRASH: I don't like her /

AHNO: Do you not /

IRASH: And to be quite honest /

AHNO: Must you /

(IRASH is afraid now.)

must you be honest /

(IRASH shrugs miserably.)

it's not necessary /

IRASH: <u>It's</u> <u>not</u> <u>my</u> <u>business</u> /

(He looks at the floor.)

is it /

(He aches with shame.)

my business? / she /

(He cannot complete his thought.)

stealing dogs I /

(He is a picture of discomfort.)

<u>hounds</u> /

(But proceeds.)

stealing hounds is one thing /

(AHNO merely watches IRASH, who develops his complaint.)

but locking up old women /

(His look is an appeal.)

I'm doing worse things every day /

(AHNO'S attention is elsewhere. He nods, bemused.)

AHNO: You see / she hasn't / has she /

(He listens.)

she hasn't run away /

(He laughs lightly.)

she makes these threats / these empty threats / in order
to humiliate me / so I beg her / so I crawl over the floor /
'stay / darling / stay' / she wants to make a slave of me /
and me /

(He bites his lip wryly.)

I don't mind slavery / I could slave for her / but it would
liquidate the passion she /

(He is amused.)

or the <u>sickness</u> / as she prefers to call it /

(He looks at IRASH.)

she feels for me /

*(IRASH barely understands his master but nods seriously. AHNO
holds him with calm gaze.)*

who am I / Irash? /

IRASH: *(Uncertain.)* Who are /

AHNO: Who? / who? /

IRASH: You are the prince of / and the bishop of /

AHNO: Yes /

(IRASH struggles to sustain his regard.)

so I cannot <u>steal</u> a hound / can I / or a wife I've seen /
I cannot steal what already belongs to me? /

*(IRASH nods his head in accord. He wants to say more, but
abolishes it.)*

IRASH: I'll go on looking /

(AHNO nods.)

it's funny but / I hear the dog bark / behind a fence
maybe / I go to the fence and /

(He shrugs.)

no dog /

(He pulls a face.)

no dog / so I knock on the door / the woman says / 'dog / what dog?' / and then I hear it / quite distant /

(He seems resigned.)

it's a stray /

(He seems embarrassed.)

a thoroughbred / obviously / but still a stray /

(AHNO goes to IRASH, and encloses him in his arms.)

AHNO: This hound /

IRASH: *(Apprehensive now.)* Hound / yes /

AHNO: Senses / exactly as madame sensed hardly a year ago / it might die of love if it were to know me / so /

IRASH: *(Seizing on this.)* It runs for its life /

(He bites his lip. AHNO does not share IRASH'S humour. IRASH nods seriously.)

I'll keep looking /

AHNO: No /

(IRASH is miserably confused.)

keep looking / no /

(He removes himself from his servant but maintains his regard.)

discover my dog / Irash /

(An old man limps on. IRASH goes to leave, then recollecting his obligations, bows to AHNO and to the old man before going out. The old man looks at AHNO for some time.)

ECZEMAS: Women / what else is there? /

(AHNO is uncritical.)

and yet /

(He waits.)

and yet /

(He watches.)

nothing else /

(And watches.)

and yet /

(AHNO confirms nothing.)

I hear you hanged someone /

(He goes towards the chair, and takes it.)

and stole a wife / all in one day /

AHNO: I flung the lever / and the wife moved in /

(ECZEMAS smiles at AHNO'S nice differentiation. The old man's eyes rest on AHNO.)

ECZEMAS: People like you / Ahno /

AHNO: Yes / they do /

ECZEMAS: Yet you lack charm /

AHNO: I feel sure / if I required charm / I could discover it /

(ECZEMAS explodes in laughter.)

ECZEMAS: That's charm /

(His gaze is silent again.)

AHNO: To be liked you must be likeable /

(He regards ECZEMAS.)

or / failing to be likeable / you might be a need /

(They study one another.)

ECZEMAS: And you /

(He might dislike AHNO.)

you are a need /

(AHNO does not reply.)

a need which they / the people / before the advent of
Ahno / did not know they had? /

(AHNO smiles thinly.)

AHNO: I walk through their brains / flinging open windows /

(He fixes ECZEMAS with his regard.)

the filth in there / the stench /

(ECZEMAS nods, as if amused.)

I hold a scented handkerchief to my nose /

ECZEMAS: And they / who smell so bad / they don't mind
that? /

(AHNO smiles, differently.)

AHNO: Why should they? / they know they stink / they also
know that I do not /

*(A mild loathing flows between them, which AHNO is content to
intensify.)*

my mother says I'm God /

(ECZEMAS resists the temptation to ridicule.)

she laboured fifteen hours for me / so /

(He shrugs.)

hyperbole comes naturally to her /

(Now he deepens his challenge.)

besides / we don't know that I'm <u>not</u> /

(ECZEMAS waits.)

we know God made the world / so he who <u>remakes</u> it /

(He tantalizes the old man.)

might be that same God / or another /

(ECZEMAS will not be drawn into a bruising quarrel. Their hostility resolves itself into laughter.)

Eczemas / how is age hurting you? / a little / or a lot? /
I so like you / and your lying is not worse / is it / not worse
than it was? /

(ECZEMAS is wounded. AHNO quotes him back to himself, witheringly.)

'women / what else is there?' /

*(ECZEMAS might reply but is stopped by the appearance of IRASH
holding in his arms a black and white spotted dog. Turning to observe
this, AHNO is strangely appalled, as if he had never expected the animal
to materialize. The dog mews, its tail sweeping from side to side.)*

IRASH: Dog /

(AHNO is gazing, and immobile.)

heavy /

(AHNO says nothing.)

heavy dog / but I thought / grab it / grab it while you can /

(IRASH is now disconcerted.)

collars / leads / baskets / etcetera /

AHNO: It's looking at me /

IRASH: That's for later on /

AHNO: I know that look /

(He gazes at the animal. The animal regards him.)

how well I know that look /

(He sustains the intensity of their mutual stare.)

the dog's a bitch /

(He waits, then leaves the room. ECZEMAS watches his departure.)

ECZEMAS: *(Still gazing after him.)* I knew Ahno as a boy /

(He recollects.)

clean / well-mannered / quiet /

(He engages IRASH.)

at first you thought / he's quiet because he's shy /

(He sniffs.)

he wasn't shy / he had concluded / correctly in my estimation / that nothing he thought could be communicated / or if it were / even dimly understood /

(He frowns.)

so he kept his mouth shut / and looked out through these eyes / these beautiful / taken-from-his-mother / eyes /

(AHNO returns. The dog fidgets.)

AHNO: So what /

(He goes directly to IRASH.)

so what if the bitch is pre-disposed to criticize /

(He relieves IRASH of the animal, taking it into his own arms.)

you excite the woman / the woman loves you / sooner or later / ask Mr Eczemas / he knows women /

(He studies the dog.)

the look /

(He creates a smile.)

the <u>look</u> arrives /

(He holds the animal firmly.)

and you must look back / never /

(And concedes nothing to it.)

aren't I right / Eczemas / when that look is laid on you / never / never / <u>lower your eyes</u> /

(He persists.)

or you're the slave of disappointment /

(The animal whimpers. AHNO interprets this as a victory and runs his hand over the head of the dog.)

there /

(And smiles warmly.)

there /

(AHNO goes out, still clasping it to himself. IRASH observes his master leave.)

ECZEMAS: *(At last.)* I thought / 'the boy's a suicide' /

(IRASH turns to ECZEMAS, who attempts a provocation.)

he should have been /

(IRASH frowns. ECZEMAS, in his passion, rises to his feet.)

<u>he should have been</u> /

(IRASH recoils.)

listen / listen /

(IRASH withdraws a pace.)

<u>listen</u> /

(ECZEMAS is confidential. He casts a look about him.)

<u>people</u> /

(He gazes into IRASH.)

what else is there? /

(IRASH shrugs. ECZEMAS is irritated by his insouciance.)

humans /

(IRASH longs to escape.)

what else is there /

(ECZEMAS writhes in his frustration.)

he doesn't like them /

(IRASH is blank. ECZEMAS senses he can only fail.)

he doesn't like <u>you</u> /

(IRASH is stung.)

IRASH: I never asked him to /

(ECZEMAS alters. He is at once benign, patronizing, a kindly smile crosses his features.)

ECZEMAS: All right / get along / you must have lots to do /

(IRASH is wary of the old man and edges out, looking back as he goes. ECZEMAS nods and smiles. The sound of the dog, excited, comes from a distance. ECZEMAS senses a figure in the dim corner, and turns.)

FALLA: I've been locked in /

(FALLA stands in a coat and holds a bag.)

for weeks /

ECZEMAS: Have you /

FALLA: Weeks /

(ECZEMAS nods.)

he says it's love /

ECZEMAS: Yes / well / it might be /

FALLA: *(Wildly.)* How can it be / how can it be love to lock a woman in a room /

(ECZEMAS is afraid FALLA is mad.)

ECZEMAS: What kind of room / a /

(Now he feels foolish.)

nice room or a /

(He falters. FALLA'S gaze is fierce.)

that's simply / simply barbaric / and /

FALLA: The boy takes out the dog / the dog's neurotic /

ECZEMAS: Yes /

FALLA: You've seen it /

ECZEMAS: Yes /

FALLA: The boy can't handle it /

ECZEMAS: No /

FALLA: He gets confused /

ECZEMAS: Yes /

FALLA: I knew / one day / he'd forget the key /

(She half-exclaims.)

I love my husband /

(ECZEMAS is apprehensive. His nod is cautious.)

and he did / he did today / so /

(She observes ECZEMAS closely.)

ECZEMAS: Today you're free /

(She nods. They hesitate.)

better hurry up because /

(He has no reason to offer.)

FALLA: How dare you think what you are thinking /

ECZEMAS: I don't know / what am I thinking? /

FALLA: You are thinking I am a mad old woman /

(ECZEMAS neither confirms nor denies.)

pity me / I am desperately in love and my body can't contain it /

(ECZEMAS does pity her. She stares at the floor.)

ECZEMAS: You don't want to leave / you want to be caught trying to escape /

(FALLA emits a small, self-deprecating laugh. ECZEMAS knows she will not leave.)

Ahno destroys everything / those who are loyal to him especially /

(FALLA observes him cannily.)

FALLA: And are you loyal? /

ECZEMAS: Me? / no /

(He pities her now.)

you should be with your grandchildren / their little weight won't injure you / whereas / with Ahno striving in your belly /

(He shrugs.)

you might dislocate your fragile bones /

FALLA: *(Who now dislikes him.)* He is subtle / Ahno / infinitely so /

(ECZEMAS laughs mildly.)

and as a consequence / I have discovered things with him no simpering grandmother will ever know /

47

(Now ECZEMAS'S laugh is one of appreciation.)

ECZEMAS: Women / what else is there? /

(FALLA deposits the bag on the floor, a predictable decision.)

FALLA: I tried to leave / if you see my husband /

ECZEMAS: I am not acquainted with your husband /

FALLA: Say she nearly / oh so nearly / but /

(She falters.)

ECZEMAS: So <u>nearly</u> <u>but</u> / I'll tell him /

(They exchange a look of suspicion, then FALLA turns to go.)

so what if he delights you in between your legs /

(She stops.)

your wasting thighs all slippery from him /

(He exclaims.)

'women / what else is there?' /

(He attacks her.)

I'll tell you what there is / there is <u>kindness</u> / and there is /

(The effort causes him to rise to his feet.)

<u>niceness</u> / and there is / there is / what he calls <u>eyewash</u> /

(He is breathless.)

<u>sentimental</u> <u>eyewash</u> / and there is / there is /

(He blurts his secret.)

kill him / you sleep with him / <u>kill</u> <u>him</u> /

(FALLA stares in horror.)

FALLA: I'd smack you /

(She is incredulous.)

I'd smack you over your face / except to do so might /

(She shakes her head in bemusement.)

fracture my wrist /

(She hates ECZEMAS.)

and I need my wrist / to pleasure him /

(She seethes. She turns swiftly and goes out.)

ECZEMAS: Tell him / tell Ahno his oldest friend is his worst /

(She is gone.)

not his <u>worst</u> / I daresay /

(He observes FALLA has left her bag behind in her indignation. He gazes.)

not his <u>worst</u> enemy /

(His eyes lift from the bag to scan the room and corridors. He then goes to the bag and unzips it. He sees what he has anticipated he might see, and stoops to remove a fragment of underwear from FALLA'S bag. He thrusts it away in a pocket as AHNO returns, swiftly.)

ECZEMAS: She wanted to leave /

(AHNO stops, his face curious, bemused.)

no / I said / he needs you /

(AHNO only smiles. His taciturn manner alarms ECZEMAS.)

I must be going /

AHNO: Why? /

ECZEMAS: *(Who does not know.)* Why / why /

(He makes a smile.)

because I don't feel safe near you /

AHNO: Safe? /

(He studies his old friend.)

how old are you / Eczemas? /

ECZEMAS: 90 / Ahno /

AHNO: Then you have had abundant safety for one life /

(ECZEMAS ponders his position. He returns to the chair and sits.)

I never speak of truth / do I / you may have noticed this /

(ECZEMAS deems it wise to nod his acknowledgement of this. AHNO suddenly is charmed by the old man.)

I'm so glad you didn't go / I ran along three corridors / me / Ahno / <u>ran</u> / I never run /

(He watches.)

I saw a pope run once /

ECZEMAS: Innocent the Fifteenth /

AHNO: Famously /

(He is dark.)

the liar / 'I'm spontaneous' / on television / obviously / 'I'm so / so very human' / the liar / the deep-dyed liar /

ECZEMAS: The people laughed /

AHNO: And clapped / they liked his deep-dyed lies /

(He smiles now.)

<u>you</u> <u>didn't</u> <u>go</u> /

(ECZEMAS is cold with fear. The dog barks distantly.)

to talk of truth it seems to me / is unnecessary / and this is where philosophy / political and social theory / argument generally / and even poetry /

(He watches ECZEMAS.)

have squandered such quantities of life and time /

(ECZEMAS faintly nods.)

no / all that is required is /

(He frowns.)

the identification / and subsequent obliteration / of the lies /

(ECZEMAS watches back. AHNO breaks the tension.)

you're tired /

ECZEMAS: Not tired / no /

AHNO: Not tired? /

ECZEMAS: Not really / no /

(AHNO judges him.)

AHNO: Not really / not really tired /

(AHNO watches, then resumes.)

the crisis / the /

(He dislikes the word.)

the /

(He smiles oddly.)

I nearly called it horror /

(He shudders.)

I hate exaggeration / horror / no /

(He corrects himself.)

crisis will do / the crisis is the discovery / the looming discovery / that without lies / man is not man at all /

(ECZEMAS stares nervously.)

ECZEMAS: And this / this / looms / does it? /

(AHNO does not reply.)

AHNO: To put it another way / he is <u>only</u> lies /

(He fixes ECZEMAS with his stare.)

lying is all that he consists of /

(He seems to suffer this, then is charming suddenly.)

or / to borrow a phrase from my old / old / so old / teacher /

(He waits.)

without lies /

(He quotes.)

'what else is there?' /

(AHNO bites his lip. He turns violently away and strides off.)

so glad I caught you /

(He is gone. ECZEMAS seizes the opportunity to clear out, but finds himself facing STRAPP, who has entered, holding his small medical bag. It is as if they knew one another, but the shock stops them. ECZEMAS speaks first.)

ECZEMAS: He has no hope /

(STRAPP frowns.)

hope / you know / hope / he hasn't got any /

(STRAPP is vague.)

STRAPP: I'm here for my wife / she /

ECZEMAS: *(As if addressing an idiot.)* <u>Hope</u> /

(STRAPP is uninterested.)

what are we without hope / <u>nothing</u> /

STRAPP: I find hope /

(He selects his word.)

burdensome /

(ECZEMAS despises STRAPP.)

ECZEMAS: <u>The</u> <u>regime</u> <u>loves</u> <u>you</u> /

STRAPP: I'm only here for my wife / she's /

(He falters.)

my wife lives here /

(ECZEMAS identifies STRAPP. He pulls the fragment of FALLA'S underwear from his pocket. He plays with it in his fingers. STRAPP is not aware of the garment's origins. ECZEMAS'S delight in his own mischief is spoiled by a fit of crapulous coughing. STRAPP seizes the opportunity to slip by. ECZEMAS recovers, and is setting off himself when PRITTY marches in, holding a gun. He shoots ECZEMAS over and over again. He departs without the least sign of exertion, reluctance or dismay. ECZEMAS is not extinguished, and remains on his knees, dimly fathoming. His hand, pressed to his wounds, is wet with blood. He looks at this hand. It occurs to him to write on the floor in his own blood. He senses AHNO has returned and is observing him.)

AHNO: I did not run /

(He approaches.)

I thought / if I am too late /

(He has no other word to offer.)

<u>well</u> /

(They are still.)

these preposterously protracted adieux delivered from the rim of his own extinction / have I the patience? /

(He coolly observes the old man.)

but you don't want to tell / you want to write /

(ECZEMAS does not confirm.)

and <u>one</u> <u>word</u> <u>only</u> /

(AHNO is moved to pity.)

oh / darling / darling man /

(He suffers for ECZEMAS.)

ridiculous the problem you have set yourself /

(He rebukes him.)

you create a gesture / an immortal gesture / you might think / when there is no word / no single word / of sufficient weight / or gravity / to fill the space of it /

(He looks at the old man, who in turn, lays his stare on AHNO, and sustains it while writing, taking more blood from his wound as he needs it. The word is short, evidently. AHNO does not examine it at once, instead retreating to the chair and sprawling in it. The sound of barking announces the return of IRASH, the animal on a lead. IRASH is unappalled by the spectacle of ECZEMAS, familiar as he now is with things here. He is about to go on his way.)

AHNO: He wrote a word /

(IRASH stops. The dog whimpers.)

love / or / hope / or / peace / or /

IRASH: *(Looking at the floor.)* <u>Cunt</u> /

(IRASH is afraid he may have offended his master.)

cunt / it says /

(Now AHNO laughs, without irony.)

it does / it says /

(AHNO'S laugh permits IRASH to laugh also.)

<u>cunt</u> /

AHNO: *(Leaping off the chair.)* <u>He</u> was not a liar / then /

(He shakes his head.)

whilst tempted by the lie / he / at the very door of death /

(He laughs on.)

<u>desisted</u> /

(He breathes in.)

<u>love</u> / etcetera / <u>hope</u> / etcetera / worthless admonitions /
no / he calls me <u>cunt</u> /

IRASH: We don't know that /

(He is hesitant.)

do we /

(AHNO looks at IRASH.)

do we know that? /

(IRASH looks at the word again.)

it doesn't say / 'you cunt' / it says /

(He shrugs.)

it just says / 'cunt' / so /

AHNO: Yes /

(He agrees with a move of his head.)

yes / thank you /

IRASH: Cunt meaning /

AHNO: Yes /

IRASH: Meaning /

AHNO: I know what cunt means /

(IRASH is silenced.)

whilst not pretending to know /

(He shares his life with IRASH for one moment only.)

the meaning of cunt /

(He laughs ironically. The point is probably lost on IRASH. AHNO moves on.)

I was presuming / wrongly probably / it was intended to be understood in its derogatory sense /

(He puts his hands to his lips.)

vain of me /

(He is disturbed.)

vain /

(He repudiates his vanity.)

and I was wrong to say there is no word / sufficient in its depth and width / to complete his gesture /

(He points to the word on the floor.)

there is /

(He shrugs.)

that's it /

(STRAPP enters, returning from his wife. He stares at the body.)

your wife /

(STRAPP drags his gaze to AHNO.)

I prefer her /

(He finds the word.)

unmodified /

(STRAPP is puzzled.)

you come here / in the guise of the physician / and with my acquiescence / you prescribe /

(He frowns at STRAPP.)

what? /

STRAPP: *(Coldly.)* I can supply you with an inventory of the drugs I /

AHNO: You see / I /

(He recollects IRASH is in the room and dismisses him with a small gesture of his fingers. IRASH takes the dog out with him.)

I feel / so long as you issue these substances to your wife / she remains your wife / it is perhaps an innocuous conspiracy /

(STRAPP is bewildered.)

STRAPP: She is depressed / deeply depressed / and /

AHNO: That is the form in which I prefer her /

STRAPP: Depressed? / you want her /

AHNO: Yes /

STRAPP: <u>Depressed</u> /

AHNO: Yes /

(STRAPP nods mildly, in a vaguely condescending manner.)

STRAPP: You have not witnessed her depression /

AHNO: *(A furious riposte.)* The depression was your marriage /

(STRAPP winces. AHNO waits.)

I am /

(He hesitates.)

so / so /

(He finds the word banal.)

<u>so</u> will do /

(And proceeds.)

so in love with this woman / I have to be not only in her nakedness /

(STRAPP winces again.)

but in the truth of her /

(He frowns.)

whatever her truth is /

(He is quite calm.)

and your substances make her a lie / as if you modelled her in wet clay with your doctor's fingers.

(STRAPP lifts his gaze to AHNO. He utters a small sound.)

STRAPP: Mmm /

(He nods, as if in accord.)

Mmm /

(He sighs. He looks at the body of ECZEMAS.)

he said / this / him / whoever he /

(He bites his lip.)

we had to kill you / because you / you have no hope /

(His smile is twisted.)

that's wrong / surely /

(He is not hostile to AHNO.)

it's hope that /

(He is reluctant to finish.)

makes you mad /

(He dares look into AHNO.)

AHNO: *(Charmingly.)* I'm not mad /

(His gaze rests on STRAPP and he nods and smiles at him, as if at a child. STRAPP thinks it opportune to escape. He withdraws backwards. He is surprised when AHNO calls out.)

I've so few friends /

(STRAPP stops, sensing this is an invitation he never sought.)

STRAPP: Same here /

(AHNO nods. STRAPP, still in reverse, edges away.)

AHNO: Oh well /

(STRAPP has gone. AHNO smiles.)

oh well / I like <u>oh</u> <u>well</u> /

(He muses.)

and <u>can't</u> <u>be</u> <u>helped</u> / I like that too /

(He knits his brows.)

and /

(He thinks.)

and /

(He finds another.)

<u>that's</u> <u>life</u> /

(He laughs with pleasure, but the pleasure drains away, as an intuition comes in its place.)

<u>mother</u> /

(He walks a little way, and stops. He emits a cry.)

<u>mother</u> /

(A figure enters, to remove the body of ECZEMAS. He stoops to take the corpse under the arms.)

my mother's ill /

(The man gazes up, stopping.)

UNDERTAKER: I'm sorry / my lord /

AHNO: *(Fiercely.)* Are you? /

   (AHNO'S response is wounding.)

   how sorry are you? /

   (The UNDERTAKER comes upright. He is not afraid of AHNO.)

UNDERTAKER: I'm sorry insofar as /

AHNO: *(Confirming him.)* Insofar as /

   (The UNDERTAKER watches.)

   good /

   (He is wary.)

   insofar as /

   (AHNO nods.)

   good / very good /

   (He smiles.)

   after all / you did not know my mother / and / had you
   known her / would you have liked her /

UNDERTAKER: I can't say / my lord /

AHNO: You can't say / and nor can I / but she was not
   likeable /

   (He watches the man, who barely nods.)

   not likeable because so great was her devotion to me / so
   absolute / so consuming of her soul / nothing remained for
   others / and I had sisters /

UNDERTAKER: *(Surprised.)* You have sisters / my lord? /

AHNO: Three /

(His gaze falters.)

Four /

(He shrugs, smiling.)

I forgot / ha / I forgot /

(He is briefly bewildered.)

I forgot the fourth /

(He is pitiful.)

the fourth whose name /

(He looks directly at the man.)

I have also forgotten /

(The man lowers his head very slightly. AHNO seems fixed in a dream. The UNDERTAKER thinks it wise to proceed.)

I don't lie /

UNDERTAKER: No / my lord /

AHNO: I could have said / Gertrude / I could have said / Jane /

(The man nods, and proceeds to pull the body away. At the entrance he stops. He looks back to AHNO.)

UNDERTAKER: Good-day / my lord /

(AHNO does not reply. The body is drawn away. AHNO thinks out loud.)

AHNO: He thinks / I saw him thinking it / 'the prince-bishop is not like us' /

(Three young priests enter. Each bears a chair in his right hand.)

that was his first thought /

(He turns to include them in his thought.)

his second thought / which I did <u>not</u> see him thinking / and which / quite possibly / has yet to resolve itself into a thought / is this /

(He smiles thinly.)

'how <u>could</u> the prince-bishop be like us?' /

(The young priests approve.)

and the third / the third thought / which follows from the second /

(He studies them.)

is what? /

LIEVENS: *(Not in the least tentative.)* 'How could we serve him if he were?' /

(AHNO is content. The three young priests gaze on him. A cry of despair comes from the depths of the house. The priests register this only in their eyes.)

AHNO: The sickness of my mother /

(He disciplines his thought.)

The mortal sickness of my mother / cannot be allowed to distract us from this conversation /

(He indicates they should sit.)

a conversation you would happily forego in order that I might sit with her / of course /

(They murmur sympathetically.)

but how can we know the extent to which our colloquy is already permeated / and intensified / by the crisis she /

(He controls his pain.)

even as we speak /

(They watch him.)

is /

(He cannot complete this thought and resorts to another.)

certainly things are altered / and in a unique way /

BURNOW: *(Staring at the floor.)* Yes /

(AHNO waits.)

yes /

(He sways on his chair.)

yes because whilst we do not welcome pain /

(He articulates with difficulty.)

neither do we / in the futile way we had become accustomed to /

(He proceeds.)

take it upon ourselves to abolish it /

(He is certain now and looks up at AHNO.)

given that / driving it from one place / it presents itself in another / no / no /

(Her cry comes again.)

we include pain in /

(And again. He winces.)

in / all things /

(The effort weakens him. He utters one last thing.)

I have no pain myself /

(And repeats it.)

I have no pain myself /

(All are silent for some time. AHNO waits.)

LIEVENS: It's the gift that no man wants /

    (He gazes at AHNO.)

    still it's a gift /

    (AHNO'S gaze encourages him.)

    a gift /

    (His own temerity frightens him but he must drive on.)

    I <u>say</u> <u>a</u> <u>gift</u> /

    (His struggle forces him to his feet.)

    and I've no pain /

    (He looks at BURNOW.)

    I've no pain either / but /

    (He aches.)

CASTOR: To <u>argue</u> pain / you cannot be <u>in</u> pain /

    (LIEVENS nods, grateful for this, and completes his thought.)

LIEVENS: A gift to him who / not suffering it /

    (He employs the word.)

    <u>beholds</u> it /

    (And looks about him.)

    <u>beholds</u> /

    (And emphasizes.)

    <u>beholds</u> /

    (He sinks back onto the chair.)

    to behold is not to look / is it /

    (He rubs his arms, as if he were chill. AHNO has heeded and appreciated his student. Only now does he leave the priests and go

into the depths of the house. They for their part remain in a state of tension which is relieved only when their eyes inevitably meet. They find themselves uncontrollably laughing, turning away, choking, laughing again. Sensing the return of AHNO, they variously thrust their fists into their mouths, hold their knees and fix their faces. AHNO, sensing their shame, is not critical, but waits, and LIEVENS is compelled to speak.)

LIEVENS: Master / we laughed /

(AHNO waits.)

and I don't know why we did /

(AHNO observes LIEVENS'S shame. He times his reply, but a cry from the house cuts him off. He withdraws for the second time. The priests are briefly still, then erupt.)

CASTOR: Why did you /

BURNOW: What did you /

CASTOR: Say /

BURNOW: Want to say that for /

(They might start to fight, but are stopped by the appearance of IRASH, with the dog on a lead. They sit, adjusting their cassocks over their knees. IRASH stares, and his stare is a rebuke.)

IRASH: Old Mrs Ahno is /

(They nod. IRASH is not mollified.)

you should be thrashed /

(They look resentful.)

how can the world be altered if those upon whom responsibility is /

(He stops. he watches.)

etcetera /

(They stare for some seconds.)

etcetera /

(He finishes in his own time.)

are the same as those whom they replace? /

(The priests sniff. IRASH rages briefly.)

so few can be trusted /

(The dog copies and barks.)

so few /

(And barks.)

all right / darling /

(And barks.)

so few / so few /

(He leads the dog away. The young priests are not rebuked. They look at the floor. They shift a little. AHNO does not return. LIEVENS'S mind is restless.)

LIEVENS: Manners /

(He frowns.)

isn't morals / is it /

BURNOW: *(Crossly.)* I'll thrash him /

LIEVENS: On the other hand /

BURNOW: Presumptuous slave /

LIEVENS: The similarity / the superficial similarity / between manners and morals / causes me to think /

(The cry of APRON briefly interrupts his thought.)

we might / if Lord Ahno should agree / teach manners / and only manners / manners being simple to acquire and /

(He is without irony.)

a perfect substitute for dignity /

(AHNO enters without haste. The priests stand and lower their heads.)

CASTOR: We hope / my lord / you may find it in yourself to forgive the adolescent laugher we /

(AHNO stops him with a lifted hand.)

AHNO: I keep a woman here /

(They dare not lift their eyes.)

I went to her / I did not go to my mother / who is dying / no / I /

(He also becomes deadly still. The priests are uncomfortable.)

went to this woman / who also may be dying / for all I know /

(He seems to invite them to respond.)

did I think by going into her /

(It is too much for BURNOW who chokes back his laughter.)

I might defy this /

(BURNOW is in pain.)

clamour of mortality /

(CASTOR is infected by BURNOW'S hysterics and shakes.)

my nakedness and hers some paltry argument against /

(CASTOR heaves out a sob as he fails to suffocate his laughter. Both he and BURNOW are wretched with shame. LIEVENS is immune to their crisis.)

LIEVENS: My lord / you /

(The other priests, out of shame and politeness, stagger away. LIEVENS watches them before resuming.)

you cannot be coerced / neither by love nor even /
I suspect / by death /

(He bites his lip.)

they can't help laughing / they /

AHNO: I like their laughter /

(LIEVENS tilts down his head.)

LIEVENS: And yet / my lord / you never laugh yourself /

AHNO: Nor do I bark / but I like dogs /

(LIEVENS is still. The cry of APRON comes again. LIEVENS cries out.)

LIEVENS: <u>Shoot</u> <u>her</u> / <u>shoot</u> <u>her</u> <u>dead</u> /

*(He is agonized by his proposition. He stares at the floor, trembling.
AHNO is moved by the young man, and goes to him. He takes his
head in his hands.)*

AHNO: The struggle against lies / which we know cannot be
won / as it intensifies / will cause you to doubt that fidelity
to me which / now / seems more important than your life /

(LIEVENS is silent.)

you will conspire against me / and when I ask / I hope
without making a degrading spectacle of myself / to be left
a little life / to keep a few sheep somewhere / you'll deny
me even that /

(LIEVENS is silent.)

you don't cry never / you don't cry never will I / never /

(LIEVENS lifts his gaze to AHNO.)

I love you for that /

(He lifts his hands away.)

love you but dog /

(He calls for IRASH.)

<u>dog</u> / <u>dog</u> /

(LIEVENS remains on his knees as the hound barks distantly and APRON cries. The two sounds fascinate AHNO, who listens, a finger lifted in the air. It is as if a significant proof were delivered to him. He smiles beautifully, as the two sounds grow in intensity. LIEVENS is captivated by AHNO and staggers on his knees the few feet that separate them. He grasps AHNO'S cassock at its hem and kisses it passionately. AHNO laughs in his ecstasy. LIEVENS rocks on his knees. PRITTY enters from one direction, IRASH from another. Silence falls as they attend, and LIEVENS is still.)

PRITTY: Things are becoming /

IRASH: So what /

PRITTY: Becoming /

IRASH: So what /

(A silence. PRITTY seethes. He looks to AHNO.)

PRITTY: Is he /

IRASH: *(Mocking.)* <u>Is</u> <u>he</u> /

(A young woman enters with the dog on a lead. She walks through, efficiently.)

is <u>he</u> / yes I am /

(He looks at PRITTY.)

<u>Irash</u> /

(PRITTY senses alteration.)

there was another Irash once /

(He looks to AHNO.)

and there is an Irash still to come / but this is Irash now / and he says /

(He gazes at PRITTY.)

so what / that <u>things</u> <u>are</u> <u>becoming</u> /

(He is lethal.)

<u>what</u> <u>they</u> <u>are</u> /

(PRITTY seems to measure IRASH. But it is LIEVENS who speaks.)

LIEVENS: With god /

(He rises to his feet.)

don't ask too much /

(He brushes down his cassock with a hand.)

he is omnipotent / still /

(He goes to leave.)

don't ask too much /

(He goes out. IRASH bawls after him.)

IRASH: <u>I'm</u> <u>not</u> <u>advised</u> /

(He fumes and repeats it.)

<u>I'm</u> <u>not</u> <u>advised</u> /

(He is self-conscious suddenly, and sensing AHNO'S regard, bows to him.)

the clever young /

(He sniffs.)

their shaved armpits / their silk pants /

(PRITTY laughs mildly.)

he calls me a log /

(And slightly again.)

he does / <u>a</u> <u>log</u> /

(IRASH smiles bitterly.)

the clever young / by <u>log</u> he means I can be walked across /

(His smile lingers.)

we'll see /

AHNO: Shh /

IRASH: We'll see /

AHNO: *(At his sweetest.)* Irash /

(He reassures his servant.)

he has his murderer /

(He looks to PRITTY.)

things are becoming / are they / but we knew this / knew things <u>must</u> <u>become</u> /

PRITTY: *(Resentfully.)* Knew it and didn't know it /

AHNO: <u>Knew</u> <u>it</u> <u>and</u> <u>didn't</u> / <u>yes</u> /

(AHNO is touched.)

yes /

(He seems to shrink and recover.)

knew / and did not know / what would be left of them / once we separated them from their lies /

(PRITTY is wan.)

PRITTY: Little /

(And looks at AHNO.)

or nothing /

(He frowns.)

and they don't create / or innovate / nor do they /

(He bites his lip.)

extemporize /

(He is uncomprehending.)

they wait / as if / the fact of waiting / would cause it to arrive /

IRASH: And does it? /

(PRITTY ignores IRASH.)

does it arrive? /

(And still ignores him.)

it being what? /

(A tremendous silence. AHNO is bemused by IRASH. IRASH senses he is mocked.)

what /

(He shakes his head.)

what fails to arrive? /

(The characteristic sound of squeaking wheels precedes the appearance of a trolley on which the body of APRON lies beneath a white sheet. The figure who pushes it fixes the brake and withdraws. AHNO'S gaze turns slowly to take it in.)

APRON: I didn't mind /

(AHNO aches.)

you not being there / I didn't mind / I thought / 'he's got a lot on his plate' /

(Now he laughs.)

and it's ugly /

AHNO: Yes /

APRON: Ugly / oh ugly / and he hates all things that are ugly /

AHNO: Yes / yes but /

APRON: You do / you know you do /

AHNO: Yes /

APRON: I thought / do what cows do / do what sheep do / go into a corner by yourself /

AHNO: *(Charmed.)* The herd goes on / the flock goes on /

APRON: Grazing /

(AHNO ponders.)

AHNO: I'd like to find your skull / lying in the grass somewhere / weak sun / weak wind / larks up there / too high to see / this song / this endless song / this skull of busted teeth / 'who was she' / I wonder / 'who was she' /

APRON: You cannot know /

AHNO: No /

APRON: Not her / not me /

AHNO: Empty skull /

APRON: Thank God /

AHNO: Empty /

(He boils.)

empty /

(He shouts to the ATTENDANT.)

hey /

(The ATTENDANT shows his face.)

throw her on a field somewhere /

(The old woman laughs.)

ATTENDANT: A field /

AHNO: An open field / but far from any footpath / or some filth will prise her thighs apart /

73

(The ATTENDANT takes his orders and pushes out the trolley. AHNO calls out in tribute.)

lay a finger on that boy /

(He laughs strangely.)

lay a finger /

(The sound of the trolley wheels fades down the corridor. IRASH and PRITTY watch AHNO. He emerges from his thought.)

I don't say where / do I / I don't say mark it on a map / the place she / and the bones / their /

(He hesitates.)

final /

(He plays with this word.)

final /

(And abolishes the word.)

no / I guard my ignorance / and lest I alter and mother-screaming run /

(He is amused.)

run like the child I was / to her rain-rinsed / sun-dried / bits /

(He looks at PRITTY who understands.)

no / of some things we must say gone /

(He urges himself.)

gone utterly / gone wholly /

(He makes the phrase.)

gone on gone /

(He is suddenly altered.)

the last man to handle her / he must be killed / surely /

(IRASH looks uncomfortable.)

or /

(AHNO is without guile.)

or he will know her whereabouts when I myself /

(He thinks fast.)

deliberately / preserve my ignorance of where she /

(But is confused now.)

that can't be /

(He looks to IRASH.)

can it / can't be /

IRASH: *(Kindly.)* We'll go together / you and me /

AHNO: *(Pleased with the proposal.)* Yes / run after him / say we /
you and me / we /

(IRASH sets off after the trolley.)

IRASH: Yes /

AHNO: *(Calling.)* I'll drive the van /

(He senses PRITTY'S peculiar regard.)

I've driven vans /

(PRITTY still watches.)

badly / badly driven / vans /

(He returns the gaze of PRITTY.)

would you want me to be perfect in all things /

*(PRITTY shakes his head, smiling. AHNO would say more but is
distracted by the appearance of FALLA, in full bridal gown and veil,
a dazzling spectacle that moves PRITTY to bow.)*

PRITTY: The costume of fecundity hangs better from the shoulders of a woman of seventy /

AHNO: Four /

PRITTY: Seventy-four / than from those plump and grinning brides officially described as nubile / if I may say so /

(He lifts his gaze to FALLA.)

and I have / on our tours / waded through much matrimony /

(He smiles grimly.)

without once encountering a wife /

(He is dark, and patient.)

AHNO: She makes me faint /

(FALLA issues a small sound in response to AHNO'S passionate oath.)

FALLA: My knees ache /

(She disparages herself with a second small sound.)

AHNO: Yes /

(He gazes on her.)

FALLA: The weight of so much satin /

AHNO: Yes / yes /

(PRITTY swiftly goes to the chair and draws it up for FALLA, who sits with exquisite decorum. The men study FALLA, infatuated.)

FALLA: On a certain date / I shall be a widow / but he can't wait / can you / darling / you can't wait /

(She smiles awkwardly.)

and my old husband / he /

(She laughs mildly.)

looks better than ever /

(The sound of the barking dog disturbs them. PRITTY tears his eyes away from FALLA, and goes to stride away, but stops. He speaks to FALLA in a tone of reverence.)

I'd fuck with you / oh / I'd fuck and fuck with you /

(AHNO accepts this uncritically.)

I wish I were Lord Ahno / he /

(He is modest in his love for AHNO.)

knows what we /

(He places his hands together.)

are afraid to know / and what we are afraid to know is /

(He shakes his head.)

Lord Ahno's ecstasy /

(PRITTY might say more, but goes out. FALLA is assured by PRITTY'S compliment.)

FALLA: Carry me /

AHNO: Yes /

FALLA: And lay me softly / softly lay me / Ahno /

AHNO: Yes /

FALLA: *(Amused.)* I should be flung / <u>flung</u> / and all this starched stuff ripped in your haste to uncover me /

AHNO: You'd break /

FALLA: I'd break /

(She is half-anxious.)

is there a priest? /

AHNO: Does one require a priest when one marries God? /

(FALLA laughs but barely. Suddenly she seems lost.)

FALLA: I'm oh / oh / old / Ahno / and dry as sun-scorched grass /

(AHNO is irritated by this repetition.)

AHNO: You are /

(He gives the word immense depth.)

old /

(He makes fists of his hands in his despair.)

and it is preferable to me /

(The barking hound comes nearer. AHNO marches out. FALLA leans on the back of the chair as the dog and her handler enter. The women look at one another.)

FALLA: *(Stricken with self-consciousness.)* I should be / I should be / what do old women do /

(QUARTZ looks without a word.)

visit museums /

(She suffers.)

sell shares /

(She emits a breathless cry and clumsily sits in the chair.)

don't laugh at me /

(QUARTZ'S regard is ruthlessly objective. She studies the spectacle of FALLA, collapsed in her gown.)

QUARTZ: I like this world /

(FALLA seems not to have heard this.)

FALLA: I had a loving husband / and I quit /

(She shakes her head. QUARTZ despises her.)

the kindness in that man /

(She shakes it more.)

oh / extravagant his kindness / and I quit /

QUARTZ: *(Affirming it again.)* I like this world /

(FALLA hears QUARTZ now.)

FALLA: This world /

(She looks at the young woman.)

<u>this</u> world / <u>this</u> world being /

QUARTZ: The world you twist and turn in /

(The words injure FALLA.)

FALLA: I do / I do twist and turn / and who are you /

(She stands up abruptly, half-staggering.)

you scrap of insignificance / who are you/

QUARTZ: Me / I'm the dog of Ahno's dog /

(FALLA is disarmed by this frank reply. QUARTZ goes to leave.)

FALLA: He wants me on a bed in this /

(QUARTZ stops.)

drowning in the satin / suffocating in the silk /

(She mocks herself.)

crack goes the starch / crack goes my hip /

(She smiles at QUARTZ.)

a ton of fabric / and in the middle of it all / my thighs /

(She assumes QUARTZ'S sympathy.)

old newspaper / my thighs /

(She looks, bemused.)

and my vulva / shrivelled fruit /

(Her gaze rests on QUARTZ.)

naked / he begs me / naked the shrivelled fruit /

(She shrugs. QUARTZ despises FALLA.)

QUARTZ: Lord Ahno is /

(She declines to complete this thought.)

Lord Ahno /

(QUARTZ looks at FALLA de haut en bas.)

do you expect him to fuck with the light off? /

(She draws the dog away. It barks. FALLA is bruised, suddenly solitary. She calls after QUARTZ.)

FALLA: Be my friend /

(QUARTZ ignores her.)

<u>be</u> / <u>be my</u> /

(The dog's bark fades. FALLA restores herself as AHNO returns, in a dark suit, immaculately cut for the occasion. He is uncritical of FALLA.)

AHNO: She was a whore / at twelve / she saw me with the dog / 'I love your dog' / she says / and it was love / I could see / more than love / infatuation /

(He smiles at the recollection.)

'look after her' / I said /

(FALLA is suspicious of AHNO.)

they share a mattress on the floor /

(AHNO senses this.)

Irash is /

(And resents it.)

you know how busy Irash is /

(FALLA stares at AHNO.)

FALLA: You <u>have</u> her /

(She is only a little critical.)

you have the little whore /

(AHNO seems depleted.)

and if it's against the law / so what / you are the law /

(AHNO will not stoop to deny her accusation.)

AHNO: Falla / how ordinary you are /

FALLA: I am / I am ordinary /

AHNO: And it would be inconsistent of me / would it not / if I complained / since this /

(He is not unkind.)

unmitigated ordinariness / is the very thing that inspires me to say /

(He indicates her bridal costume.)

<u>pristine</u> / <u>pristine</u> <u>is</u> <u>your</u> <u>decay</u> /

(He rejoices. Then expunges it, seeing her frown.)

and then / to see you / flounder /

(He is utterly bereft.)

<u>flounder</u> / in the contradiction /

(He sniffs.)

which is not contradiction /

(His smile is thinner than ever.)

oh /

(He turns to see STRAPP enter.)

two gods / surely /

FALLA: *(Seeing STRAPP.)* Darling /

AHNO: Never could create /

FALLA: Darling / darling /

(She is a spectacle of disintegration.)

AHNO: A thing of such cruel beauty / no /

(Now IRASH enters holding FALLA'S suitcase.)

the ordinary is /

(STRAPP is uncertain if he might embrace his wife, but she has run into his arms.)

<u>indispensable</u> /

(STRAPP is looking at AHNO, for permission, but he is not sure for what. As they hesitate, IRASH throws down the suitcase with a clatter, and withdraws, bowing to AHNO all the while. He passes LIEVENS, who arrives and stands attentively.)

STRAPP: I box /

AHNO: Yes /

STRAPP: Box me / then /

(AHNO shakes his head with disdain. Leaving his wife, STRAPP goes and collects the suitcase, fixing its catches.)

Lord Ahno will not box /

(STRAPP glowers.)

but I am boxing him /

(His bitterness overflows, and he goes towards AHNO, stopping only when he senses a movement on the part of LIEVENS. LIEVENS has removed an automatic from beneath his cassock. He stops. He thinks better of his impulse. He goes to take his wife away, but she seems fixed to the floor. He looks back at AHNO.)

FALLA: What a love / oh what a great / great love /

(STRAPP is perfect in decorum, waiting for her to make her departure. AHNO cannot reply. They go out. LIEVENS replaces the gun in his clothes.)

LIEVENS: My Lord Ahno did not say yes /

(AHNO glances at him.)

he might have done / through cracked lips croaked some /

(He improvises.)

'darling / never / ever / can I forget the beautiful' / etcetera /

(He smiles.)

some lie that might have eased her death /

(He is patronizing.)

easy / except you never falsify your feelings /

(AHNO detects the direct address but says nothing of it.)

AHNO: We don't say darling here again / the word /

(LIEVENS bows his head in accord.)

LIEVENS: I always thought it / if I may say so / impoverished /

AHNO: Not in my mouth /

LIEVENS: In your mouth / no /

(AHNO'S regard is severe and LIEVENS avoids it. He resorts to a light observation.)

he did not want her back / I thought /

(AHNO does not assist him.)

a certain fatigue crept over him at the prospect of /

(He half-laughs.)

more compromise / more self-abnegation /

(He nods, knowingly, bows, and goes to withdraw. As he does so, he spins on his heel and confronts AHNO with his anger.)

why does God fix his heart on such a / such a /

(He aches.)

such a poor thing /

(He shakes his head.)

and call it <u>darling</u>? /

(AHNO does not assist LIEVENS, who arrives at his own conclusion.)

with God /

(He looks up now.)

don't ask too much /

(He shrugs. He seems to appeal to AHNO.)

I say that often / and / it is no disparagement of him /

(He struggles to comprehend.)

and it's not as if / if she were beautiful / beautiful and profoundly intelligent /

(He thrashes his mind.)

the <u>darling</u> / <u>darling</u> / <u>darlingness</u> /

(He is bold.)

would satisfy me in the least /

(All he can do now is to laugh loudly and uncannily, at the conclusion of which he drags out the automatic and fires it into the ceiling.)

<u>that's</u> <u>you</u> /

(And fires again.)

<u>that's</u> <u>you</u> <u>I'm</u> <u>killing</u> /

(The shots arouse the dog, which barks distantly. AHNO knows it is possible LIEVENS will turn the gun on himself, and is not unduly perplexed. He walks a few paces and looks back.)

I am your superior / in all things / superior / superior /

(The hound, released from its lead, races in, barking.)

yes /

(And goes to AHNO.)

<u>oh</u> <u>yes</u> /

(As LIEVENS plunges through his emotions, QUARTZ enters, holding a broken lead.)

QUARTZ: Sorry / sorry / she /

(She slaps her thigh.)

<u>here</u> / <u>here</u> /

(QUARTZ laughs.)

she is so /

(The dog is smothering AHNO.)

<u>down</u> / <u>down</u> / I said /

(AHNO is not disturbed by the dog's devotion, but lifts her in his arms and carries her away. QUARTZ watches, charmed. LIEVENS resents his redundancy. He glares at QUARTZ.)

LIEVENS: Fuck now /

QUARTZ: *(Who has not heard him.)* She loves him /

LIEVENS: Fuck / I said /

QUARTZ: She loves <u>me</u> but /

LIEVENS: Fuck / fuck /

QUARTZ: *(Still gazing off.)* When he's around /

LIEVENS: <u>Fuck</u> / <u>fuck</u> <u>with</u> <u>me</u> /

(Now she hears and turns a cruel face to him.)

QUARTZ: Silly /

(LIEVENS is punctured. His mind reels.)

LIEVENS: All right / say darling /

QUARTZ: What? /

LIEVENS: Darling / say /

QUARTZ: Why? /

LIEVENS: <u>Say</u> / <u>say</u> /

(He is on the verge of tears. QUARTZ will not satisfy him. He is utterly downcast.)

why won't you say? /

(She shrugs. He stares at the floor. Slowly, his senses return. He discovers he is still holding the gun, and stuffs it away.)

I like you /

(QUARTZ is indifferent to this news.)

I like you /

(He sniffs.)

and there are so few people /

(The word hurts him.)

so few /

(He stares at the floor.)

I can even /

(He shrugs.)

<u>tolerate</u> /

(And smiles.)

in <u>my</u> <u>vicinity</u> /

(QUARTZ looks at him dispassionately.)

QUARTZ: Funny word /

(He looks up.)

<u>vicinity</u> /

LIEVENS: You like words / do you? /

QUARTZ: *(Yielding him nothing.)* I like that one /

LIEVENS: *(Sweetly.)* It means /

QUARTZ: I know what it means /

(He nods.)

<u>vicinity</u>

(He looks, in awe of QUARTZ.)

I never had one /

(He nods again.)

until I came here / or if I did / nobody noticed it /

(She is not indignant.)

they just walked in /

(She nearly laughs.)

saying /

(She does laugh.)

<u>fuck</u> /

(And looks at LIEVENS, who is ashamed.)

Anyway / I've got one now / and my vicinity is /

(She lacks a word. LIEVENS offers.)

LIEVENS: Strictly /

QUARTZ: <u>Strictly</u> / yes /

(She smiles naturally.)

but for the dog /

(LIEVENS nods. QUARTZ is apparently cheerful and goes to stride out. A thought stops her. She appeals to LIEVENS.)

don't poison her /

(LIEVENS is shocked by her dread, and can only shake his head. She hesitates, twitches her hands, a picture of vulnerability, briefly. She goes.)

LIEVENS: Darling /

(LIEVENS hardly knows he has uttered the word, and is perturbed. His reflections are curtailed by the appearance of CASTOR and BURNOW, in battle dress.)

BURNOW: You don't go out /

CASTOR: Michael /

BURNOW: Do you /

CASTOR: Or rarely /

BURNOW: Very rarely /

LIEVENS: I've been ill /

BURNOW: So very rarely out / nowadays /

CASTOR: Of course / you're senior /

BURNOW: You're senior / but still /

CASTOR: This seniority /

BURNOW: We all get ill /

CASTOR: Does not entitle you /

BURNOW: I'm ill now / aren't I? /

CASTOR: To shirk responsibility for /

LIEVENS: *(Indignant.)* <u>Shirk</u> /

CASTOR: Shirk / yes / I don't know any other word /

BURNOW: Very ill /

CASTOR: For managing the outings /

> *(LIEVENS looks persecuted.)*

> because you do so few / John and I / we do more /

> *(LIEVENS is unabashed. He adopts a principled tone.)*

LIEVENS: You two / you /

BURNOW: *(Resentfully.)* 'You two' /

LIEVENS: *(Persisting.)* I think it could be said /

BURNOW: '<u>You</u> <u>two</u>' /

LIEVENS: Are comfortable with /

CASTOR: *(Gravely.)* Michael / we are not /

> *(LIEVENS senses his error.)*

LIEVENS: Forgive me /

CASTOR: Comfortable with /

LIEVENS: Forgive me / I said /

> *(CASTOR'S resentment is in the word.)*

CASTOR: The <u>outings</u> /

> *(LIEVENS aches. BURNOW walks a little.)*

BURNOW: No / I'm very ill / I get sore throats / and vomiting / horrible vomiting /

> *(LIEVENS affects sympathy.)*

> that's the physical /

LIEVENS: Yes /

BURNOW: The physical / however /

CASTOR: We can tolerate the physical /

LIEVENS: *(Predicting.)* Is not unrelated to /

BURNOW: Not unrelated / no /

LIEVENS: The moral /

BURNOW: The moral / so why don't you /

(His argument is cut off by the appearance of AHNO, and from other directions, PRITTY and IRASH. AHNO lets the silence persist, taking a few paces in one direction, then the other, before addressing them.)

AHNO: The wounding and the healing come from the same place / has this ever been understood? /

(He waits, not expecting an answer.)

it is now /

(He regards them.)

they talk of leaving the earth / the astronauts / they say the earth is beautiful / but only from a distance /

(He waits.)

the one who does the wounding / him it is who heals /

(He is passionate.)

this is the place / there is no other /

(He is conciliatory.)

and you are tired of wounding / I see it in your faces / tired of wounding / yes /

(He looks up at them.)

what use are the astronauts? / do they not understand this is the place? /

(He scoffs.)

pity the astronauts / but from the death side /

(He is grave.)

their evasiveness / unforgivable /

(And walks, and stops.)

the time came / did we not know this / in the place where things are really known / not in the brain / therefore / never in the brain /

(He lets this idea settle.)

the time came /

(He weighs the words.)

to cease providing / and to take away /

(He is demonstrative.)

and you are tired / I see it in your faces / tired of taking away /

(He lifts his hands.)

but the time came /

(He looks into them.)

as it came for others / and did they not feel / in their agony /

(He stops in his surge.)

I must not speak for them /

(He is pained.)

I must not /

(And lifts his gaze.)

though I know them / I must not say /

(He shakes his head.)

their futility / they alone /

(And shakes it more.)

they alone /

(He states calmly.)

and it was not futile / whilst it rose and fell in futility / it was not /

(He shrugs.)

their time came /

(He resumes his theme.)

the healing starts even as the wound has passed the place /

(He senses their willingness may be waning, and abandons his style, with a disarming sincerity.)

I can speak in other languages /

(They seem hurt, rebuked. He watches them.)

you remember humour / you remember how all things came wearing humour like a cape / and you saw I never laughed / you saw I was /

(He dares them.)

beautifully humourless /

(He is swift.)

here's a joke /

IRASH: *(As if stung.)* No /

(They all laugh at IRASH'S impertinence.)

no /

(He is pained.)

my lord can tell a joke /

(He bows.)

but he must not tell one /

(He goes on.)

whilst he has the best joke ever told / I beg him not to tell it /

(He shrugs, uncomfortably.)

I can't say why / yes / I can /

(He is certain.)

it would be as if he took off all his clothes /

(No one dissents from or endorses this. IRASH continues.)

I didn't understand that / what my lord said / not one word /

(He frowns.)

the words <u>said</u> /

(He frowns more deeply. He cries out.)

the words said what they said / but /

(He flicks a hand in frustration.)

that wasn't what I heard /

(He struggles.)

I heard /

(He fails. He abandons.)

anyway / no jokes / my lord / I beg you /

(He recovers himself, and wittily goes onto his knees.)

I implore him /

(He seems to knock his forehead on the ground.)

I <u>implore</u> /

(AHNO is charmed by his servant and raises him affectionately. He takes his cheeks in his hands, and embraces him. The others, led by CASTOR, clap. They depart, inspired, but LIEVENS lingers.)

LIEVENS: So /

(The boots of the men fade down the corridor.)

so /

(He affects to ponder.)

<u>meaning</u> is less /

(He chews his hand.)

less than the sum of the <u>speaking</u> / and /

(He chews on.)

and / the <u>manner</u> of the speaking /

(He looks to AHNO.)

is that correct /

(AHNO does not reply. IRASH looks murder at LIEVENS.)

is that /

(He is stopped by the swift appearance of QUARTZ, elegant in black, and her hair cut costly.)

QUARTZ: Dwarf / shh /

LIEVENS: I am not a /

QUARTZ: Shh / dwarf / shh /

(LIEVENS is puzzled.)

LIEVENS: I am five foot eleven /

QUARTZ: Shh /

LIEVENS: Inches / high /

QUARTZ: *(Sweetly.)* Dwarf /

(She comforts him.)

<u>dwarf</u> /

(LIEVENS ceases to protest, and creates a smile, uncomfortable but defiant.)

AHNO: She lay with dwarves /

(IRASH laughs.)

she did / and of dwarves she says /

(He looks at QUARTZ.)

oh / she is full of praise /

(LIEVENS is embarrassed by his apparent misunderstanding of QUARTZ, who now laughs lightly, gazing at LIEVENS.)

LIEVENS: I am / to my own detriment / it would appear / humourless /

(He grimaces.)

still /

QUARTZ: *(Kindly.)* Dwarf /

LIEVENS: *(Nodding faintly at her.)* I have to say / so awful is our task / I would think myself diseased if / while giving pain / I laughed /

(He looks at AHNO.)

my lord does not /

(He looks at the floor.)

I have not seen one photograph / even from his childhood / in which the vaguest smile can be discerned /

(LIEVENS senses his destruction, but the moment is disrupted by the appearance of STRAPP, in shorts and boxing gloves, a spectacle which, after a few seconds, causes IRASH to burst out laughing.)

IRASH: He's a boxer / I said so / didn't I / the day I first set eyes on him / that doctor has been taught to box /

(He shakes quietly. STRAPP is dead still, staring at the floor. The facts dawn on AHNO.)

AHNO: My darling's dead /

(STRAPP confirms nothing, nor moves his eyes.)

and he wants to /

(He alters his assessment.)

he <u>must</u> /

(He looks for a word.)

inflict his /

(QUARTZ removes an automatic from her skirt.)

his /

(He knows the word.)

<u>loathing</u> / on me /

(After some seconds, STRAPP lifts his eyes to AHNO.)

QUARTZ: Lay a finger on that boy /

(She cocks the gun.)

I'll blind you /

(STRAPP hears this but his regard is fixed.)

STRAPP: Blind me /

(STRAPP surges towards AHNO but IRASH comes smartly forward and throws a punch to STRAPP'S jaw. The old man staggers back. QUARTZ cannot keep from emitting a high-pitched laugh, partly disbelief. AHNO has not moved. STRAPP recovers and comes back to the attack on him. Again, IRASH directs a blow to STRAPP'S jaw, with the same result. Now no one laughs. Slowly, STRAPP restores himself, and goes back into the attack. Without pleasure, IRASH sends him sprawling again.)

LIEVENS: <u>Stop</u> <u>that</u> / <u>stop</u> <u>that</u> /

(STRAPP is on hands and knees.)

AHNO: Let him hit me /

(QUARTZ cannot believe AHNO has said this. IRASH bows to AHNO and stands back. STRAPP is still able to stand and fight. He recovers. He gathers himself up. He does not immediately go into the attack. He regards AHNO warily.)

you are ridiculous because you love / and I am never ridiculous because I never have /

LIEVENS: Yes /

(LIEVENS regrets this spontaneous syllable, heard but not registered by AHNO.)

AHNO: Whether she was entitled to your devotion /

STRAPP: *(Curtly.)* <u>Doesn't</u> <u>matter</u> /

AHNO: Or my infatuation /

STRAPP: <u>Doesn't</u> <u>matter</u> /

AHNO: *(Thoughtfully.)* No /

(STRAPP seems about to launch himself but is overcome by a consuming thought.)

STRAPP: She was on her way to you / for the tenth time on her way to you /

(AHNO is unsurprised.)

and slipped /

(He inhales to control his pain.)

ten times to a man who /

(He is overwhelmed.)

<u>ten</u> <u>times</u> /

(He shakes his head wearily. IRASH takes the initiative and going to the old man, unlaces his boxing gloves. STRAPP does nothing to resist, and is pitiful. LIEVENS occupies the silence.)

LIEVENS: I endorsed Lord Ahno's statement that he has never loved / not from a critical position /

(He fetches the chair and places it for STRAPP.)

the <u>reverse</u> /

(The old man sits.)

only a culture / such as that from which we have so nearly emerged / sickly with eroticism on the one hand / and crippled with an ungovernable sentimentality on the other / could fail to be in awe of a man who repudiated <u>love</u> / in order to better understand /

(He nods his head passionately.)

what <u>love</u> might be /

(He dares himself.)

or if it needs to be at all /

(And affirms his daring.)

<u>yes</u> / <u>yes</u> /

(He looks to them all, bleakly.)

it is so damaged / it is so damaged / love /

(He catches sight of the mess of STRAPP.)

behold /

(He waves a hand to the old man.)

<u>the</u> <u>wreckage</u> /

(No one dissents.)

no / it's evident to me we / we / need not suffer the humiliations of this /

(He shrugs.)

and other / archaic sentiments which in any case are /

(He finds the word in his need.)

<u>embroidered</u> <u>instincts</u> /

(He is embarrassed by his own genius and laughs weakly.)

one might change the words / we might call love / I don't know / some other thing / but /

(He rocks on his feet. His hands are nursing his face.)

why / why / when we could /

(He laughs again, weakly.)

abolish the whole /

(He need not finish. Again he indicates STRAPP.)

<u>behold</u> <u>the</u> <u>wreckage</u> /

(He is falsely modest.)

speaking for myself / I have no desire to be subject to these humiliations which describe themselves /

(He hits the word.)

<u>preposterously</u> /

(He shakes his head with contempt.)

as <u>ecstasies</u> /

(Again he invokes STRAPP.)

<u>behold</u> <u>the</u> <u>wreckage</u> /

(He is luminous.)

no / no / this revolution will not as revolutions always do /

(He smiles.)

exchange one word for another / it will /

(He seems to cease suddenly, but it is a rhetorical gesture.)

abolish the thing the word failed to describe in the first place /

(He notices the intensity with which QUARTZ observes him, and goes closer to her.)

how beautiful this woman is /

(He nods sagely.)

are we to say to her / go down into the street / and fascinate / and suffer the consequences of this fascination / birth / age / oh / just do what /

(He flicks a hand.)

they all did / no / something new /

(He might weep.)

oh / something new /

(He is pleased with this impromptu performance.)

we beg /

(Correctly, he bows to AHNO, who plays with LIEVENS.)

AHNO: And beauty / beauty itself /

LIEVENS: *(Seizing on this.)* Yes / yes / that too /

(He shakes his head, again with a superior smile.)

I've read the poems / I've seen the statues / thank you /

(He repeats his plea.)

I beg /

(LIEVENS is certain of his powers, even complacent. QUARTZ and IRASH stare, half-bewildered, but they are not his audience.)

I beg /

(Distantly, the hound barks. For some time no one speaks. AHNO is moved by his disciple. He can only utter his own doubt.)

AHNO: I don't know /

(He smiles oddly.)

I <u>don't</u> <u>know</u> /

(He is energized, but his regard remains on LIEVENS.)

I <u>pulled</u> <u>the</u> <u>lever</u> / oh / years ago / they said / 'he'll never do it / he's far too kind / Ahno' /

IRASH: I remember /

AHNO: You remember /

IRASH: The bastard /

AHNO: He was / he was /

STRAPP: *(Pathetically.)* I'm cold /

AHNO: A killer of children / so /

STRAPP: <u>I'm</u> <u>cold</u> /

AHNO: Not difficult /

(IRASH slips off his own jacket.)

to pull the lever /

(And drapes it over the old man.)

later /

(The dog barks more anxiously.)

QUARTZ: *(Crossly.)* She's no good with that dog /

AHNO: <u>Later</u> /

QUARTZ: Is she? /

(An unusual whine is heard. QUARTZ is incensed and walks some paces to the door.)

don't hit that dog / don't dare /

(There is silence now.)

AHNO: Later / I could not bear / even on the outings / to watch /

(He shrugs.)

I cared too much for my own feelings /

IRASH: It was not your job /

(AHNO regards IRASH.)

AHNO: Thinking / I might coarsen them /

IRASH: It was not Lord Ahno's job /

AHNO: *(As if puzzled.)* Coarsen my feelings /

(He frowns.)

as if God recoiled from /

(Spontaneously he puts his fingers to his mouth and whistles.)

his own acts /

(The dog bounds in, and runs to AHNO, who scoops her into his arms. She licks and laps. A girl appears, holding her lead, and waits.)

LIEVENS: And if God did / if God did recoil from his own acts /

(He plays with his fingers.)

would that /

(He watches AHNO.)

fastidiousness / be an indictment of the acts /

(He dismisses the idea.)

hardly /

(He is complacent.)

hardly at all /

(He is suddenly engulfed by horror and turns on them all.)

<u>we</u> <u>are</u> <u>all</u> <u>so</u> <u>afraid</u> <u>of</u> <u>the</u> <u>future</u> /

(Except for AHNO, who strokes the dog, the whole room seems afraid of LIEVENS'S vehemence. He senses this.)

<u>but</u> <u>we</u> <u>are</u> <u>making</u> <u>the</u> <u>future</u> /

(He looks from one to the other. He smiles. He consoles.)

perhaps it isn't fear / perhaps it's only /

(The dog whines and mews.)

<u>hesitation</u> /

(As if without thinking, LIEVENS drifts towards AHNO.)

I have seen it in a horse / this hesitation / a horse ridden at a fence /

(He lifts a hand to the dog.)

it must be jumped / the fence /

(He gazes at the others.)

the horse knows this / it knows it will perish if it does not abolish hesitation at the very instant hesitation /

STRAPP: *(Out of silence.)* Horses /

LIEVENS: Insinuates itself /

STRAPP: <u>Don't</u> <u>jump</u> <u>fences</u> /

(LIEVENS is patient, apparently.)

LIEVENS: Forgive me / I have seen horses /

STRAPP: *(With contempt.)* Men <u>make</u> <u>them</u> /

(LIEVENS is lost for words. STRAPP gets up wearily. For a moment he leans on the back of the chair, then, recovering, he offers IRASH

his jacket. IRASH takes it back. The old man limps away, the boxing gloves swinging from a hand.)

JUTLAND: *(Calling out.)* <u>Trick</u> /

(They seem oddly shocked by her insouciance.)

<u>that</u> /

(She stares after him.)

<u>trick</u> /

AHNO: *(Lifting one paw of the dog.)* Her nails /

JUTLAND: *(Reproved.)* Oh yes /

AHNO: Need /

JUTLAND: Yes /

(AHNO waits.)

AHNO: Need to be clipped /

JUTLAND: I said yes / didn't I? /

(JUTLAND'S insolence shocks the room, but not AHNO, who laughs. JUTLAND shakes her head over STRAPP.)

that trick / oh /

(She flicks a hand.)

<u>dignity</u> <u>trick</u> /

(Now LIEVENS laughs.)

it is / it is /

(She is palpably upset, AHNO goes to her.)

it is a trick / everything is /

(She half-sobs. AHNO puts the dog on the floor.)

and they call us /

(She stamps her foot.)

what is that word /

AHNO: Coercive /

JUTLAND: Coercive /

(She seethes against STRAPP.)

that /

(She points after him.)

that's /

(She loses the word at once.)

what / what is that /

LIEVENS: *(Patiently.)* Coercive /

JUTLAND: That's / coercive /

(She does not remove her eyes from the direction, but speaks to AHNO.)

when can I have a gun? /

AHNO: Now / if you want / ask Irash /

JUTLAND: Thank you /

AHNO: *(Setting off.)* And cut her nails /

JUTLAND: I will do /

AHNO: Carefully /

(PRITTY follows AHNO.)

JUTLAND: I'll be careful /

(She attaches the dog to the lead. IRASH pulls out a number of automatics from his clothes. He selects a lightweight version, and adjusts its mechanism. QUARTZ frowns.)

QUARTZ: I hesitate to /

(She hesitates. She looks to LIEVENS, who last invoked the word.)

and having <u>hesitated</u> / dare to criticize Lord Ahno's judgement /

(She dares.)

is it wise to give a child a /

(QUARTZ hears herself and is shocked.)

'is it wise?' /

(She shakes her head.)

I sound like a / like a /

(She jeers at herself.)

like everything I hate /

(She admits her exasperation.)

<u>she</u> <u>would</u> <u>have</u> <u>shot</u> <u>the</u> <u>old</u> <u>man</u> <u>in</u> <u>the</u> <u>back</u> /

JUTLAND: *(Indignantly.)* <u>I</u> <u>wouldn't</u> <u>have</u> /

(She glares at QUARTZ.)

I despised him /

(QUARTZ returns her glare.)

I despised him /

(They watch.)

I <u>only</u> <u>despised</u> /

(JUTLAND abandons the contest and stalks across to IRASH, receiving from him the smallest gun.)

LIEVENS: The judgements of Lord Ahno can / from time to time / seem arbitrary / even whimsical /

(IRASH stuffs the remaining weapons away.)

with the passage of time / however / a certain / and I have to say / inexorable / logic / could always be identified /

(Thrusting her gun in her belt, JUTLAND turns to the dog.)

at least until now /

JUTLAND: I'm cutting your nails /

(The dog resents.)

I <u>am</u> / I <u>am</u> /

(She tugs on the lead.)

LIEVENS: The death of the old woman /

(JUTLAND stops.)

the so-decayed and so / so very / cantankerous / old woman Lord Ahno /

(He lifts a hand vaguely.)

Lord Ahno <u>what</u> /

(He turns to IRASH.)

what did he do with her /

(He jeers to himself.)

I hesitate /

(And laughs.)

I hesitate to speculate /

(JUTLAND fires a single round from her little gun. An awful silence fills the room. LIEVENS, unable to grasp his situation, puts a hand to his chest. IRASH stares. QUARTZ twists. The dog whimpers.)

LIEVENS: *(Fixing her with his gaze.)* Stupid /

(He is ghastly.)

un / utterably / stupid /

JUTLAND: *(Horrified.)* That was a mood /

(She turns a frightened face to QUARTZ.)

that was a mood / it wasn't calculated /

(Recovering from his shock, IRASH drags the chair to LIEVENS, who sinks into it.)

LIEVENS: Not calculated / she says /

JUTLAND: It <u>wasn't</u> / <u>it</u> <u>wasn't</u> <u>calculated</u> /

LIEVENS: It was / but not by you /

(IRASH goes to pull away the clothing from LIEVENS.)

don't touch / don't touch me you /

(LIEVENS winces with pain. IRASH removes his hand. In a spasm of disgust, JUTLAND flings her little gun away. It clatters over the floor.)

QUARTZ: *(To JUTLAND.)* Cut her nails now /

(JUTLAND looks to QUARTZ, whose gaze is fixed on the mortally wounded LIEVENS.)

LIEVENS: Carefully / as Lord Ahno told you to /

(JUTLAND is pale with horror, but undiminished. She turns to take away the dog, then stops and rebukes the dying man.)

JUTLAND: 'I hesitate to speculate / I hesitate / I hesitate' /

(LIEVENS turns a sickly gaze on her.)

he did though /

(She looks at QUARTZ, without shame.)

he did / didn't he? /

(She sniffs, defiantly, and draws the dog away. IRASH, suddenly galvanized, surges out, leaving QUARTZ alone with the dying man. She goes closer.)

LIEVENS: Giving her the gun / he knew / he knew what she would do with it /

(QUARTZ nods.)

if not today / tomorrow /

(She nods again. He is nearly humorous.)

and I thought / 'he's dislocated' /

(He suffers.)

'he's disturbed' /

(He stares at QUARTZ, dumbfounded.)

he wasn't though /

(She can only shake her head in accord.)

he never is /

(He appears consumed by disbelief. AHNO enters, unhurriedly, from a direction which prevents him being visible to LIEVENS. He goes to the chair and leans on it. For a time he is silent.)

AHNO: You want a thing /

(He looks at the back of his hands, pensively. LIEVENS, fading, glimpses the hands, so close to his face.)

oh / how you want it /

(He waits.)

after a time / you discover you are alone in wanting it /

(He looks down at LIEVENS' head.)

entirely alone /

(He ponders. He is certain.)

and let's be clear / there is a solution to this /

(He nods.)

fatuous <u>wanting</u> /

(Now he places his hands on LIEVENS' head.)

how brilliantly he articulated this / I heard it / and it entered me / <u>the</u> <u>solution</u> /

(His body affirms it.)

brilliant / brilliant / youth /

(He throws back his head and laughs peculiarly.)

you <u>abolish</u> <u>wanting</u> /

(He is serene.)

and with the death of wanting comes the death of <u>lack</u> /

(He affirms it with a passionate nodding of his head.)

I said 'put on the wedding dress' / she said 'I'm 70' / I said /

(It pains him to utter it.)

I said / '<u>because</u> you are 70 /

(He is saddened.)

put on the wedding dress' /

(He frowns.)

she <u>looked</u> /

(He smiles, wanly.)

that vapid / vapid / look /

(LIEVENS dies silently. JUTLAND enters, renewed, mature, in a perfect costume. She attends.)

to think we might be gratified /

(He lifts his eyes to her.)

oh / how we plead / and strain / and kill for it /

(He nods.)

whilst knowing / all the time / we will be denied /

(He asserts joyously.)

it is in <u>the</u> <u>lack</u> that we are beautiful /

(He shakes his head over LIEVENS.)

beloved youth /

(And applauds JUTLAND.)

<u>perfectly</u> <u>shot</u> /

(He smiles at her.)

is my dog near /

(JUTLAND speaks in a new voice, refined and confident.)

JUTLAND: Is your dog /

AHNO: Near /

(They know this routine.)

JUTLAND: Not near / no /

AHNO: Not near /

JUTLAND: Dead and buried / your dog / will you have another /

AHNO: I won't have another / no /

(They laugh at the repetition of the catechism. QUARTZ kisses JUTLAND on the cheek, a discreet formality, before going out. JUTLAND is quite still, observing AHNO.)

I was sick this morning /

(She lifts her head.)

sick again /

(She waits.)

and I've been with nobody / no man / no boy /

(And waits.)

say if you came to me by night / say <u>if</u> /

(He is silent, but it is not confirmation.)

so I have nobody's child /

(She is glad of this.)

<u>nobody's</u> /

(She laughs, mildly.)

and if it could be proved the child was somebody's / still I'd say / it is nobody's child /

(She looks at AHNO as if at herself.)

when it's due / I'll know / and find some corner of a field / come rain or snow / I'm doing that / Ahno / and if it dies / and if I die / so / <u>so</u> /

(She screams.)

<u>I</u> <u>can't</u> <u>be</u> <u>touched</u> /

(And laughs.)

this field / it might be where your mother's bones /

(She screams again.)

<u>I</u> <u>can't</u> <u>be</u> <u>touched</u> /

(And is recovered at once.)

lie / or do not lie / no / the magpies / they let nothing lie / where her bones were /

(She is without humour.)

casually deposited /

(She affirms.)

it is insignificant if in my agony I cry /

(She cries it.)

'doctor / the pain is more than I can bear' /

(AHNO admires.)

insignificant /

(She stares at AHNO.)

and if / seeing the body of nobody's child lifeless on the grass / some dog-voiced policewoman declares / 'that perfect infant need never have died' /

(She iterates.)

insignificant /

(Her look is a command.)

you will not let them near me / Ahno /

(He need not confirm this.)

the long tongues of their looking lapping / lapping /

(She giggles.)

lapping the dew /

(She throws back her head.)

I don't mean dew /

(She is dark.)

I mean blood / don't I / lapping the blood from my white thighs /

(She reiterates.)

you won't / will you /

(She reveres him.)

we hate it / oh / how we hate the near /

(She waits a long time.)

I was sick this morning /

(They are in absolute unanimity.)

sick again /

*

EXQUISITE

Characters

FEVER	A Male Serf at 70
RIBBONS	A Lord at 40
THOMA	His Wife at 70
BLEW	A Female Serf at 50
UNBORN	A Female Serf at 18
EGYPT	A Male Serf at 18
FORJAX	The Son of Thoma at 40

1

*A man enters. He wears an apron and carries a pair of boots. He sits.
He polishes the boots.*

FEVER: Serf /

> *(He works on.)*

> dom /

> dom /

> dom /

> *(He is assiduous.)*

> serf

> *(He lifts one to the light.)*

> <u>dom</u> /

> *(Satisfied, he places it on the floor and works on the second.)*

> <u>dom</u> /

> *(The brush goes fast.)*

> <u>dom</u> /

> serf / dom / serf / dom / serf /

> *(He inspects the boot.)*

> <u>dom</u> /

> *(He is satisfied.)*

> serf / serf /

> *(A woman strides in, lavish, immensely clean.)*

> <u>dom</u> /

THOMA: You /

FEVER: *(Yielding her the chair.)* <u>Serf</u> /

THOMA: <u>May</u> /

FEVER: <u>Dom</u> /

THOMA: <u>Not</u> /

(She glares at FEVER, who observes her without flinching.)

FEVER: Those who anticipate / welcome / and even facilitate / great changes / apparently fatigued by the situation as it is / describing it as stagnant / sterile / and so on / a suffocating burden on their talent and ingenuity / wanting the fields even to erupt in paroxysms of repudiation / and ancient trees to fling themselves out of the ground where they have stood the strain of gales for generations / crashing down with impacts so shattering the porcelain is set trembling in the cabinets of museums distant by many miles / museums that must be / and cabinets that must be / pulverized in the great and necessary abolition of all things still and sterile that suffocate the ingenuity of / the talent and the ingenuity of / those who /

(He ceases. Their regard is sustained in silence.)

their talent / and ingenuity /

(And is sustained longer.)

THOMA: I said you may not /

FEVER: They /

THOMA: <u>Cease</u> / <u>with</u> / <u>me</u> /

(FEVER heeds her.)

FEVER: Are on the move /

(THOMA is resolute.)

and nothing will / or can / obstruct their passage / or satisfy their appetite / dead children / of their own making / notwithstanding /

(THOMA stands.)

THOMA: *(Assuming his consent.)* Good /

(She goes to leave, but stops, as if he might speak for himself.)

FEVER: All we can do is wait / resistance / argument / wild gestures of resentment / assassination / for example /

(They gaze.)

fatuous /

(THOMA waits.)

in the end / after all the noise has died away / the noise of torture and of murder / it becomes apparent that / after all / they had no talent / nor any ingenuity /

(He almost smiles.)

beyond that which existed already /

THOMA: *(Charmed.)* Serf /

FEVER: Dom /

dom /

dom /

I'll come tonight /

THOMA: *(Disdainfully.)* Tonight /

FEVER: Tonight / my lady /

THOMA: Tonight / will you / you'll come tonight /

(She sneers.)

tonight I'm doing trivial things /

FEVER: Tomorrow / then / tomorrow night /

THOMA: You are wilfully / or stupidly / misapprehending me /

FEVER: Stupidly /

THOMA: Stupidly misapprehending me / look at me /

FEVER: I am / I am looking at you / my lady /

THOMA: You are looking at me / and telling me you will wait until tomorrow night before /

FEVER: *(Reminding her.)* I said <u>tonight</u> /

THOMA: Before /

FEVER: <u>Tonight</u> / I said /

THOMA: Before /

FEVER: To which you said / 'tonight I'm doing trivial things' /

THOMA: *(Wrecking his argument.)* <u>Before</u> / <u>before</u> /

   <u>before</u> /

   (Her mockery succeeds.)

FEVER: <u>Now</u> / then / <u>now</u> / and not tonight /

   (She is triumphant. They gaze. FEVER is infatuated, but delays his move to her.)

   *y*ou are all dressed up /

   (She bites her lip.)

   dressed up for an occasion / and on your way to / or /

   (He is bemused.)

   halfway through / this occasion / you want to feel my /

   (He sways slightly on his feet.)

THOMA: I want to feel <u>your</u> / yes /

FEVER: My still-living /

THOMA: Your still-living /

FEVER: Travelling /

THOMA: Your still-living travelling down my thigh / I do /
yes /

(He goes to move again. THOMA, closing her eyes, insists.)

say we cannot cease /

(Her eyes are closed still.)

say /

say /

(He declines to conform.)

say you cannot cease with me /

*(FEVER darkens with a thought he is reluctant to express, but does
at last.)*

FEVER: Ask me afterwards / if I can cease with you /

*(The effect of this is to destroy THOMA'S ardour. She opens her eyes.
She creates a gesture in her shoulders of timeless regret. FEVER is
moved by her, but they cannot act now.)*

THOMA: I wonder why /

why you /

I wonder why /

*(She drifts out. He is still, perhaps ashamed. Suddenly, THOMA
strides back in, stops and seems to have to utter. Her hands describe
this. She fails. She goes out equally swiftly. For some time FEVER
waits, then returns to the chair, picks up the second boot, and studies
his workmanship. An old woman enters.)*

2

She looks at him. He regards her.

BLEW: You were born of a lord /

    (FEVER shakes his head.)

    there's lord in you / Fever / and it's why no one likes you /

FEVER: Oh / am I not liked? /

BLEW: You're false /

FEVER: False / am I? /

BLEW: False as a lord /

    (She gazes. He looks at her a long time.)

FEVER: Strange as it may seem to you / I try /

    (He ceases, smiles oddly.)

    try? / I <u>exert</u> myself /

    (She looks with some sympathy at him.)

    to eradicate all falseness from my life /

    (BLEW smiles.)

BLEW: I believe you / but you can't help yourself / and no more can they /

    (FEVER resents BLEW'S verdict. He looks away, as if to conclude it.)

FEVER: The serfs will die / and the lords / the lords who were once serfs / they will die / and the serfs who have lord in them /

    (He regards her.)

    or were born of lords /

    (She studies FEVER.)

them too /

BLEW: So you say /

FEVER: I do say /

(His look lingers.)

and in one place / and with one cry /

BLEW: What cry? /

(He smiles. He stands.)

the way you clean boots / Fever / it's /

(She shakes her head.)

not as if they were your own/

(FEVER lifts the boots, gazes on them. He bites his lip, thoughtfully.)

FEVER: Serf /

(He turns them to catch the light.)

<u>dom</u> /

BLEW: Yes / but /

FEVER: Serf /

(He looks from the boots to BLEW.)

<u>dom</u> /

BLEW: I'm a serf /

(By way of reply, he smiles. BLEW is combative.)

<u>I'm</u> a serf / but /

(She shakes her head, not without menace, but chooses not to pursue the argument. FEVER calls out as she goes.)

FEVER: The <u>cry's</u> <u>why</u> <u>me</u> /

(BLEW stops.)

I said they'll cry one thing / the lords / the serfs / as they die / one thing only / and unanimously /

(BLEW looks at FEVER.)

what thing / you said /

(He shrugs. He turns up the boots.)

today I did not polish the soles / and I can say to you /

(He smiles for himself.)

it troubles /

(He nods fervently.)

<u>mildly</u> / <u>mildly</u> troubles /

(And looks at BLEW directly.)

my conscience /

(BLEW is not amused.)

BLEW: These things are noticed /

FEVER: Yes /

(BLEW is reluctant to abandon her quarrel with FEVER, but decides to quit. His call stops her.)

Blew /

(She does not turn her face to him.)

there <u>is</u> no reckoning /

(His opinion is unbearable to her. She strides away, but is obliged to stop and create a half-curtsy for a young man who, ignoring her, goes to the empty chair and sits.)

3

FEVER: My lord / I was bringing the boots /

(He makes an obeisance with his head.)

things /

(He kneels, and begins to unlace the dirty boots of his master.)

and by things / I must mean people /

(He swiftly and adeptly unthreads the laces.)

obstructed me /

(He tugs the boot.)

first / it was your wife /

(He pulls it off.)

after your wife / the old woman Blew /

(And begins to unlace the next.)

and they had things to say /

(He works swiftly.)

not any old things /

(He tugs.)

'have you fed the chickens?' / 'will it rain today?' /

(He tugs harder.)

nothing like that /

(The boot comes off.)

big things / the changing nature of the erotic in society / labour and its obligations /

(He reaches for a clean boot.)

as a consequence / I regret to say / I neglected to polish the undersides of your walking boots /

(The boot goes on.)

of course / the undersides are <u>cleaned</u> /

(He looks up briefly.)

only not <u>polished</u> /

(He works at the laces.)

it's a strange thing / this / but whilst a trivial conversation might be perpetuated /

(He pulls tight.)

ever so long / whilst an action / unrelated to it / is simultaneously carried on /

(He ties the laces.)

the moment a profound / or controversial / subject /

(And goes to the next.)

<u>swims</u> <u>in</u> / as it were /

(And goes to the next.)

everything is dislocated / the boot brush remains suspended in the air /

(He emits a small laugh. The second boot comes off. He sets it aside and goes to the second clean boot.)

RIBBONS: <u>Don't</u> /

(The single syllable stops FEVER in mid-action.)

FEVER: Don't what / my lord? /

RIBBONS: *(Icily.)* Polish the undersides of my boots /

(Time passes. FEVER stares at the floor.)

it's unnecessary /

(FEVER seems to struggle with this concept, and might reply in many ways. He settles for the simplest.)

FEVER: But you are a lord / my lord /

RIBBONS: I am /

(He watches FEVER.)

and you / you are serf /

FEVER: I am a serf / my lord /

RIBBONS: And I wonder why my wife should enquire of a serf /

(He shrugs.)

I cannot precisely remember what it was that she enquired of you /

(FEVER is still.)

something / something /

(He is irritable.)

the erotic something /

(And more so.)

in society / you said / erotic something /

(FEVER seems obtuse.)

erotic what /

FEVER: *(Lifting his gaze at last.)* My lady thinks I know things /

RIBBONS: And do you? /

FEVER: I know how to be a serf / my lord / as very few serfs do /

(He shrugs very slightly.)

which is why / on principle / it matters that I should not only clean / but polish / the undersides of my master's boots /

(RIBBONS is complacent.)

RIBBONS: All right / polish them /

FEVER: *(Dragging on the boot.)* I am grateful to my lord /

(He begins the lacing.)

my lord's lady / in conformity with the prejudice of this and / for all I know / every society /

(He tugs and knots.)

thinks the old are wise / and it is tempting / obviously / to satisfy this appetite for knowledge by uttering some random cliché /

(He tests the knot, then satisfied, the lifts his hands away.)

this I try not to do /

RIBBONS: Very wise / my wife is not susceptible to clichés /

FEVER: Is that so? /

(He scrambles to his feet.)

unfortunately / so often we find the clichés to be true /

(RIBBONS looks at FEVER.)

RIBBONS: Speak one /

(FEVER shrugs.)

speak a cliché /

(FEVER chooses at random.)

FEVER: 'Some people are born lucky' /

(RIBBONS seems to study FEVER.)

RIBBONS: Hard to disagree with that / speak another /

FEVER: 'He had it coming to him' /

RIBBONS: *(Nodding.)* Yes / yes / and another /

FEVER: *(A moment's reflection.)* 'There's more to it than meets the eye' /

(RIBBONS nods again. He seems irritated now.)

RIBBONS: Go on /

FEVER: Another? /

RIBBONS: Another cliché / you /

FEVER: *(Hesitating a moment only.)* 'What cannot be cured' /

RIBBONS: *(Irritably.)* 'Must be endured' /

(He is indignant.)

I know / I know these things /

FEVER: Of course / my lord / they are clichés /

(RIBBONS regards FEVER curiously for some time, a scrutiny FEVER finds uncomfortable. He goes to collect his master's discarded boots.)

I will have these cleaned / and ready for my lord when he /

RIBBONS: I understand my wife /

(FEVER can only gaze at the floor.)

FEVER: I am /

(He is briefly dislocated.)

I /

(He raises his eyes to RIBBONS.)

am glad to know my lord is /

RIBBONS: Coming to you / as she does / I also feel a powerful desire to confide in you /

FEVER: *(Sensing danger.)* If my lord were to confide in me /
    I should cease to be a serf /

RIBBONS: *(Seizing on this.)* Yes / well / yes /

(FEVER is on guard.)

and is there not something preposterous about you being a
serf at all? /

(FEVER watches.)

always I thought / he / you / the old man with whom it is
impossible to find fault / who is scrupulously dutiful / he
is /

(He flicks a hand.)

a serf for all the wrong reasons /

(His gaze penetrates FEVER, who is patient.)

FEVER: And the right reasons / my lord / what might they
    be? /

(RIBBONS is unwilling to be drawn. FEVER is again slow to proceed.)

my family /

RIBBONS: I know all about your family /

FEVER: *(Nodding to this.)* Forever serfs / my family /

(He feels the gaze of RIBBONS. He dares himself.)

and yet / were serfdom not ingrained in me /

(He is provocative and knows it.)

still / I might think /

(He nods again.)

serf /

dom /

dom /

(He reiterates.)

serf /

<u>dom</u> /

(He frowns.)

cleans the soul /

(RIBBONS is not hostile.)

RIBBONS: And it follows / I daresay / if you could be <u>me</u> / you wouldn't be /

(FEVER is content to smile. RIBBONS goes out calling.)

we're out till late /

FEVER: Late / yes /

RIBBONS: *(Disappeared now.)* Not very late /

FEVER: Not very /

(He is dead still, holding the boots.)

not very /

4

FEVER goes to the chair, sits, and extending his legs, gazes at the ceiling. In the depths of his thought, he forgets he is holding the dirty boots. They clatter to the floor. This does not distract him, nor is he surprised when THOMA sweeps in, stops, poses with her hands on her hips and smiles.

THOMA: <u>Headache</u> /

(FEVER draws down his eyes.)

headache so not going /

(He receives this information, but persists with his thought.)

FEVER: This propensity of theirs for <u>making</u> <u>lists</u> /

(THOMA is patient.)

it's as if / by itemizing the satisfactions of their civility /
they demonstrated their entitlement to perpetuate
themselves / as if the sheer bulk of their pleasures could
only overwhelm those who / blindly and stubbornly / it
seems / repudiate them /

(He laughs faintly.)

'this cannot last' / you say / and they recite their virtues /
as if it guaranteed them against violation /

(He shakes his head slightly.)

'that's not a wall' / I say / 'it's a list' /

(Now he looks directly at THOMA.)

THOMA: Poor darling / he said /

(They gaze.)

poor darling /

(And sustain their gaze.)

FEVER: If he comes to kill me / I shan't resist /

(THOMA is critical. She is about to speak, stops, starts again.)

THOMA: That's inconsistent /

FEVER: Yes /

(THOMA glares at him.)

THOMA: To say /

(She falters to her irritation.)

to say / as you do /

FEVER: It's inconsistent / my lady / yes /

THOMA: You are my husband's property / and then /

FEVER: Thoroughly inconsistent /

THOMA: To steal his wife /

FEVER: I did not steal his wife / his wife /

THOMA: *(Furiously.)* All right / all right /

(They glare in silence. FEVER persists.)

FEVER: His wife /

THOMA: I said all right /

(She frowns. She emits a sob.)

now I have got a headache /

(She laughs. She is a picture of pain and love.)

just say / because I want you to / just say / when you set eyes on me / you thought /

(She giggles.)

you thought / 'if I stole wives' /

(She stares at him, biting her lip.)

'if' /

(And commands him.)

'if' /

(She is severe.)

'if I was the sort who' /

FEVER: I am / I am the sort who /

(They gaze into one another.)

nevertheless / it was you /

(She frowns exquisitely.)

you who /

THOMA: Me /

(She affirms.)

me / me who / me /

(She is moved.)

I was wet to my knee /

(Her look is full of love.)

to my knee / and I was 70 /

(She laughs, protests, mocks him.)

you are pedantic / so pedantic / who cares if it was me or /

(She flicks a hand impatiently.)

who cares / who cares /

(She is suddenly dark, hearing a sound.)

he's not gone /

(She stares at FEVER. Her body is stiff.)

he's not gone /

(She surges out. FEVER, in his own time and deliberately, retrieves a boot. He seems about to clean it, but stops and is utterly still.)

5

FEVER: To want to know /

(He harks.)

why /

why know /

why know what you need not know /

why /

(The faint cry of THOMA, distantly. FEVER is still for a long time.)

so now you know /

(Her cry comes again.)

you know /

(He seems to struggle to compose himself.)

you know and /

(He senses the presence of another. A youth is revealed, still as FEVER himself.)

EGYPT: Hear that? /

FEVER: What? /

(EGYPT raises a finger to command silence. THOMA'S cry comes.)

EGYPT: That /

(And again.)

<u>that</u> /

(FEVER stands. He might strike EGYPT.)

he's having her /

(EGYPT pulls a face, thinking FEVER might share his prurient pleasure. FEVER is icy.)

FEVER: Yes /

(He looks at the floor.)

desire overcame them /

(He is perfectly constrained.)

simultaneously /

EGYPT: Never mind us /

FEVER: Never mind you / never mind me /

(EGYPT sniffs, resentfully.)

EGYPT: We don't exist /

(FEVER is still with menace.)

FEVER: We exist / but as a barn door does / and if I wanted my wife / I should not let a barn door inhibit me /

(EGYPT'S frown becomes a scowl.)

my lord is free /

(Patiently, FEVER returns to the cleaning of the boot.)

whether some of this freedom is conditional upon you /

(He stops.)

or me /

(He bites his lip, pensively.)

suffering this freedom / and being seen to suffer it /

(He frowns.)

I couldn't say / not being free /

(He looks at EGYPT.)

EGYPT: I don't get you / Fever /

(FEVER stands, seething.)

FEVER: You do / you do / you liar / you do <u>get</u> <u>me</u> /

(EGYPT is afraid.)

EGYPT: All right /

(He shrugs.)

things to do / I /

(And shrugs more.)

things to do /

FEVER: *(Resuming his seat.)* <u>Do</u> <u>things</u> /

(EGYPT turns to escape. FEVER is calm at once.)

no / no /

(EGYPT stops. FEVER is benign.)

it's impossible the resentment of a slave like you should constitute a fraction even of the pleasure my lord might find in taking his wife against a tree /

(They gaze.)

impossible /

(FEVER smiles.)

one might as well offend the worms / or / or /

(He shrugs.)

make the blackbirds shriek with indignation /

(He lifts the brush.)

but how should I know / I'm not free /

(EGYPT starts to go.)

serfdom /

(And stops.)

serf /

(He looks at FEVER, curiously.)

<u>dom</u> /

<u>dom</u> /

<u>dom</u> /

(FEVER'S look on EGYPT is lingering. EGYPT retreats. FEVER does not resort to brushing but gazes into space.)

6

FEVER: How will they be known? /

(He answers himself.)

by their words / obviously /

(He frowns.)

these words will be made out of other words / or parts of them / mutilated and stitched together so as to be familiar /

(He ponders.)

vaguely / vaguely familiar / and therefore / less menacing /

(He is still a long time.)

these new / and scarcely new / words / will be descriptions /

(He smiles wanly.)

for a while /

(He looks at the ceiling, bemused.)

for a while / <u>descriptions</u> <u>for</u> <u>a</u> <u>while</u> /

(He waits for himself.)

after which / they will become /

(He is darkened.)

<u>reasons</u> /

(His face is a mask of stone.)

and you / who did not know the word even /

(He waits.)

months ago /

(And waits.)

will say / 'so this is the reason' / as you are drowned in a hole /

(He does not reflect long. His mask is flung off with a cruel laugh.)

and the smile / I did not mention the smile /

(He stands.)

the smile that goes with the word /

(He goes out with the boots.)

7

Three serfs driving rakes. They traverse, stop, and let the rakes fall. They variously stretch or fidget.

BLEW: We say nothing /

(She gazes over the land.)

when we talk / we say nothing /

(She massages her neck.)

I met a priest / he said <u>discern</u> /

(They idle.)

I do / I said / I do discern / and because I discern / I know we say nothing /

(They idle longer.)

he thought /

EGYPT: <u>Serf</u> /

BLEW: Serf / he thought /

EGYPT: She won't know <u>discern</u> /

(They idle. As if time had expired, BLEW bends to retrieve her rake. UNBORN follows suit. THOMA is discovered, observing them.)

my lady /

BLEW: *(A faint genuflection.)* My lady /

(Now EGYPT picks up his rake. The three line up to continue their task, but EGYPT seems distracted. He cannot go on. He stifles a laugh by rubbing his nose. BLEW looks at him reprovingly. Still he dithers, his shoulders shaking. THOMA goes to leave, stops.)

THOMA: I dreamed of terrible trouble /

(They rake in line. EGYPT sniffs.)

not caused /

(And rake.)

terrible / terrible / trouble /

(They rake.)

with no cause /

BLEW: *(Stopping her rake.)* My lady has listened to Fever /

(She shrugs.)

Fever says nothing is caused /

(THOMA looks critically at BLEW.)

THOMA: Does he /

(She seems to ponder the idea.)

that's silly /

(BLEW nods.)

BLEW: Things happen / he says / then people look for a cause /

(She studies THOMA.)

silly /

(They are all still, uncomfortable.)

THOMA: If the roof falls in /

(She shrugs.)

BLEW: There must be rot in the beams /

THOMA: Obviously /

BLEW: Obviously / yes /

(EGYPT sniffs. THOMA goes to leave. With immense difficulty, UNBORN speaks.)

UNBORN: That's not the cause /

(THOMA stops.)

THOMA: *(Bemused.)* The rot's not the cause? /

(UNBORN shakes her head, painfully self-conscious.)

then what is the cause? /

(UNBORN shakes her head again. She bites her lip.)

the woodworm have /

(Again she shakes.)

the rain and the woodworm /

(UNBORN lets out a cry. She seems to sway on her feet.)

UNBORN: The lord did not look at the beams /

(All three of her hearers digest UNBORN'S remark for some time.)

THOMA: Yes /

(She is patronizing, unintentionally.)

yes /

(And looks at the girl.)

well / that is a /

143

(She shrugs.)

that's also a cause /

(UNBORN twists and shakes her head at the same time.)

he forgot / this / this / <u>negligent</u> <u>lord</u> /

(UNBORN stares at the ground.)

UNBORN: He did not /

(She becomes still.)

he did not / forget /

(THOMA studies UNBORN a while. BLEW decides to resume the raking, to spare them further discomfort. EGYPT copies at once. THOMA and UNBORN are still for some time, until UNBORN also resumes. At last THOMA withdraws. The serfs rake.)

BLEW: Today / I <u>discern</u> /

(They move in a line.)

things were said /

(They rake offstage. A young man enters. His gaze follows the serfs. Summoned, FEVER arrives, and attends.)

8

The young man senses the presence of another, and turns to regard him. The regard lingers.

FORJAX: *(At last.)* Says my mother / 'discuss this / discuss this with someone who's wise' /

(His look travels FEVER.)

'And who might that be' / says I / 'this one you call wise?' /

(Again he looks over FEVER, critically.)

you / she says / you /

(FEVER makes no form of reply.)

five children she had / I'm the last /

(FORJAX waits.)

not only the last /

(He smiles oddly.)

the one who survived /

(He waits, longer, then pours out his complaint.)

so we're close / very close / to my detriment <u>very</u> / as a child / a young child / I stood watching as she showed off her clothes / my opinion was critical / 'say yes' / she said / 'say yes or no' / if I said no / off came the garment / she was naked / briefly naked / on went another / 'say yes / darling / say yes or no' / we were close / very close / to my detriment <u>very</u> / 'and the colour / what of the colour?' / I said white / only white / so her wardrobe was white / entirely / and remains white / so far as I know /

(He is grim-faced.)

I asked to inspect it / the wardrobe /

(He chews.)

no / she said /

(FORJAX waits. FEVER is scrupulous.)

FEVER: My lady your mother is the wife of /

(FORJAX closes his eyes in his impatience.)

FORJAX: Be wise / for God's sake /

(FEVER is briefly rebuked, then essays again.)

FEVER: When a woman marries /

FORJAX: *(Irritated.)* Be <u>wise</u> / be <u>wise</u> /

(FEVER calculates.)

145

FEVER: You think / you think / my lady my mother / she is 70 /

(FORJAX stares at the ground.)

70 / what can she /

(FEVER manipulates the tension.)

in her white clothes / on those white sheets /

FORJAX: <u>Wiser</u> /

FEVER: *(Emboldened.)* While he / white with his longing / widens her knees /

FORJAX: *(Severely.)* <u>Wiser</u> / please /

FEVER: You think / if any man should kiss her there /

(He scrutinizes.)

it's me /

(FORJAX is perfect in stillness. FEVER proceeds.)

and it's not as if he's old and dusty / quite the reverse /

(FEVER dares.)

he's vigorous / and /

(He gauges his effects.)

brings her to her ecstasy many times a day /

(FORJAX maintains himself.)

you think /

you think /

my lady my mother / all this <u>doing</u> / all this <u>doing</u> / and <u>being</u> <u>done</u> <u>to</u> /

(He observes, waits, goes on.)

what is it she dreads to hear / this thing that silence would make audible? /

(FEVER will go no further. FORJAX emerges from his stillness with a forced smile.)

FORJAX: <u>Wisdom</u> /

(FEVER barely inclines his head.)

wisdom / and we must be friends /

FEVER: *(Who feared this.)* I am a serf / my lord /

FORJAX: *(Abolishing this.)* Assuming that /assuming and including that /

(He is certain.)

<u>friends</u> /

(FEVER is now on the defensive.)

FEVER: My lord / I /

FORJAX: You don't want to be /

(FORJAX'S gaze is cruel.)

you don't / do you /

FEVER: If I may be allowed to remain / as I am / <u>friendless</u> / I should be in your debt / my lord /

(He raises his eyes to the YOUNG MAN.)

I find all forms of intimacy incompatible with the proper discharge of my functions /

(They regard one another.)

moreover / if my lady your mother was correct to call me wise /

(He finds a smile, strange, thin.)

such wisdom as I have /

(He is modest.)

I never found through conversation /

(FORJAX likes FEVER more for this, but can do nothing but walk slowly and thoughtfully in a circle, at the end of which he stops, creates a small gesture of acquiescence, and goes out. FEVER is relieved to have escaped an unwelcome intimacy.)

serf /

dom /

(He tastes the syllables.)

serf /

serf /

dom /

(He is dimly aware of THOMA, who has entered.)

9

THOMA: Thank you /

(FEVER looks at THOMA.)

what you said / he said / it took away his pain /

(FEVER inclines his head.)

what did you say? /

(He looks at THOMA a long while.)

FEVER: The kind / the kind who made their kindness a vulgarity / they will become unkind /

(He frowns.)

and their unkindness will exceed the unkindness of those who were called unkind in the first place /

(THOMA is patient.)

to such an extraordinary degree people will say / 'give us the unkind back / for all they did was look the other way / whereas these /

(FEVER shakes his head.)

these / oh / <u>these</u>' /

THOMA: *(Biting her lip.)* All right / don't tell me /

(She smiles.)

what my lover reveals to my son / and what my son says of his mother /

FEVER: *(Cutting into her.)* My lord your husband needs to know /

(THOMA anticipates, and blanches.)

or /

(FEVER frowns.)

or the need is mine / <u>I</u> need him to know / because /

(He looks boldly at her.)

if he remains in ignorance of the fact I have his wife /

(Her eyes narrow.)

I have this over him / and a serf who has this thing / or any thing at all / over his master / is no serf / tell him / and if he /

(FEVER shrugs.)

<u>lets</u> <u>it</u> /

(He smiles grimly.)

my serfdom is preserved / as is his mastery / I plough his ground / and his wife / I plough her / but /

(She looks witheringly.)

at his behest /

(THOMA is not less clever than FEVER, and watches.)

THOMA: When you /

(She only half-despises him.)

an old man /

(FEVER watches.)

are inside me / an old woman /

(She measures her effects.)

you are further into me than any young man ever got /

(He heeds her closely.)

and we both know why /

(She sneers, but uncritically.)

it's treachery /

FEVER: How well I'm known to everyone / and how little I appear to know myself /

(THOMA is wistful.)

THOMA: Very well / I'll get permission /

(She smiles.)

and if he does not murder you / and does not murder me / let us see what permission does to your /

(She suddenly experiences a pang of longing.)

I love you / Fever /

(Her head twists on her neck.)

your /

(She throws away the thought.)

you may not cease /

(Her severity is intimidating.)

you may not cease with me /

(She goes out. If FEVER might say more, he refrains.)

10

As FEVER gazes after THOMA, a figure races in from his blind side, deals him a blow across his head, and hurtles out again, without ceasing in his velocity. FEVER sways from the concussion, and sensibly sits on the ground, his hands to his head. He remains so for some time. He is observed.

UNBORN: They hate you /

(FEVER is too shocked to respond. For a while UNBORN cannot articulate.)

but you /

(She gnaws.)

you don't hate them /

(She writhes.)

and you never will /

(FEVER is head in hands, nauseous.)

no matter how horribly they wound you / you will not pollute your soul by /

(By way of reply, FEVER turns a ghastly face on the young woman, who, seeing the blood on him, winces.)

FEVER: Please /

(She bites a hand.)

it is humiliating to hear you /

HOWARD BARKER

(He wipes his hand on his clothes.)

ascribe these perverse /

UNBORN: Perverse? /

FEVER: Perverse / yes / perverse /

(He winces now.)

characteristics / to me /

(UNBORN is wounded by FEVER'S repudiation of her faith.)

characteristics which / holy or not in your estimation /

(He tries to stand.)

are worse / vastly worse /

(He sinks back onto his haunches.)

than the contempt I am accustomed to /

(UNBORN gawps, then flees. FEVER shouts.)

I've <u>no</u> <u>humility</u> /

(The shout hurts him. He is surprised to see RIBBONS enter, dragging UNBORN tightly by her wrist. He looks at FEVER.)

RIBBONS: *(Icily to UNBORN.)* Help him /

(She is timid, confused.)

help / you know / <u>help</u> /

(UNBORN approaches FEVER.)

<u>wash</u> <u>the</u> <u>man</u> <u>and</u> <u>bandage</u> <u>him</u> /

(She tears out. RIBBONS watches FEVER.)

I've got another one /

FEVER: Another one? /

(He tries to stand, sinks. RIBBONS gestures him to stay as he is.)

another what / my lord? /

RIBBONS: Cliché /

(And at once recites it.)

'Straight roads lead nowhere' /

FEVER: *(Weakly.)* Is that a cliché / my lord / I don't recognize it / but /

RIBBONS: Here's another /

(He proceeds as before.)

'If you must read books / read them with your eyes shut' /

(FEVER is puzzled and suspicious at once.)

FEVER: Now that / I don't think / is a cliché /

(They watch closely. FEVER, through his dizziness, senses RIBBONS'S intention.)

are there others? /

RIBBONS: Lots /

FEVER: I wonder if I will recognize a single one of them /

RIBBONS: Try this /

(FEVER is apprehensive.)

'Knock at the front door / enter by the back' /

(FEVER nods, as if he appreciated this also. RIBBONS is patient.)

FEVER: Each one of these / these / clichés which are /

(He looks up at his master.)

scarcely clichés at all /

(UNBORN returns with a bowl and cloth. With an irritable gesture, RIBBONS stops her.)

seems to me to / simultaneously to / repudiate the obvious / and incite deceit /

(He keeps his eyes on RIBBONS.)

perhaps that is the reason they /

(He is reluctant to criticize.)

fail to be clichés / in the time-honoured sense /

(RIBBONS lets time pass.)

RIBBONS: Have you ever loved a woman / Fever? /

(FEVER takes the question seriously.)

FEVER: I may have thought so at the time /

(RIBBONS absorbs this, and turns to go. He stops.)

RIBBONS: This hitting of you / I think it will occur again /

FEVER: *(Coldly.)* Yes / my lord /

RIBBONS: And it won't be on my orders /

FEVER: No / my lord /

(RIBBONS hesitates, marches out, as BLEW enters. Seeing the condition of FEVER, she lets out a cry.)

BLEW: Oh you / oh /

(She takes the bowl from UNBORN and goes to attend to FEVER.)

FEVER: I want to be nothing / I want to find nothing / and be nothing /

BLEW: You can't be nothing /

FEVER: To be silence / and to move in silence /

BLEW: *(Washing his head.)* You can't / nobody can /

FEVER: *(Wincing.)* I find a lord / the nearest lord / I think / I'll be the serf to this lord / and if this lord is brutal / and a fool / so much the better / I will serve a fool /

BLEW: He is not a fool /

FEVER: He is not / no / nor is his wife /

BLEW: It's you who is the fool / Fever /

(Furiously, FEVER grabs the hand with which BLEW washes him.)

FEVER: I am a fool / am I / if I do not hate / a fool if /
enslaved / I do not grind my teeth / and whine / and
whine at my enslavement /

(He stares wildly at the old woman.)

every act of yours is grudged / every grain of wheat you /
every nut / and every fruit you /

(He is wounding.)

soddened in resentment /

(And still grasps her.)

extraordinary you can lift the basket that you carry / your
misery doubles its weight /

(He frees her. She shakes her wrist.)

BLEW: You'll be hit again / Fever /

FEVER: I will / will I? /

BLEW: *(She pities him.)* Not with my encouragement /

FEVER: I believe you / Blew /

(He smiles wanly.)

but of course / you'll understand why the act took place /

*(The implied rebuke is not lost on BLEW. She withdraws, calling to
UNBORN as she goes.)*

BLEW: We're in the flat field /

(UNBORN does not follow BLEW. She dithers, wanting to speak.)

UNBORN: You can't be hit again /

FEVER: No /

UNBORN: Can you / at your age / you /

(FEVER, still seated, folds his hands and stares into the distance.)

I should go /

(She does not.)

Blew / she / if you hang back / she /

(Her little laugh is false.)

gives you a slap /

(Still she delays. FEVER senses what it is she requires of him, and is mildly irritated.)

FEVER: The walls are very close / what's written on them / you can read it for yourself /

(UNBORN is hurt, but must be content. She goes out, and immediately returns, aggressive in her resentment.)

UNBORN: Murderer /

(FEVER is not provoked. He turns his face to UNBORN.)

FEVER: Murderer is not written on the wall /

(UNBORN seems to boil. She emits two syllables.)

UNBORN: Not yet /

(He studies her discomfort.)

FEVER: Not yet written on the wall? /

UNBORN: Not yet a murderer /

(She stares wildly.)

you /

(FEVER nods, patronizingly.)

all the same / you know a murderer is what you are /

(FEVER affects to contemplate this. UNBORN is relieved.)

and to spare the one who / or the <u>many</u> / God knows how many you might cruelly kill /

(She is radiant in her theory.)

you turn your back on freedom / and live a slave's life when you never were a slave /

(She admires. FEVER is grim.)

EGYPT: *(Calling.)* The flat field /

UNBORN: *(Swiftly to FEVER.)* It's our secret /

(FEVER is resigned.)

no one but me will ever know what a merciless killer you might have been /

EGYPT: *(Entering.)* <u>The</u> <u>flat</u> <u>field</u> /

(He sets his hands on his hips. UNBORN goes out, unintimidated. EGYPT is about to follow.)

FEVER: Was there a good man / ever / even one / I ask myself this / and all the synonyms / the synonyms for good / profuse / why? /

(EGYPT looks blank.)

why this profusion / it can only be because the word is holed and leaks / and the synonyms are heaped against it / lest the word should sink /

(He smiles oddly at EGYPT.)

heaps of synonyms / suspicious / don't you think? /

(EGYPT shrugs, and turns to go.)

<u>you</u> <u>know</u> <u>what</u> <u>I</u> <u>mean</u> /

EGYPT: *(Turning back.)* Syn / what? /

FEVER: *(Simply.)* You know what I mean /

(He smiles at EGYPT.)

you don't know the words / still / you know what the
words mean /

(EGYPT goes out.)

11

*Sensing movement behind him, FEVER turns to meet RIBBONS, THOMA
and FORJAX, as they idly perambulate. He bows from the waist.*

RIBBONS: Head all right now? /

FEVER: Head better / my lord /

RIBBONS: Not hit again / I hope? /

FEVER: Not hit again / my lord /

RIBBONS: In that meaningless and completely unprovoked /

FORJAX: We don't know that /

*(RIBBONS looks patiently at his son-in-law, who is arm-in-arm
with his mother.)*

we don't know / do we / we <u>cannot</u> know / if it was
unprovoked? /

(A brief, odd silence elapses.)

only / only /

THOMA: *(Coldly.)* His name is Fever /

FORJAX: Thank you /

(He smiles.)

only <u>Fever</u> himself might know if the attack was
unprovoked /

(He gazes on FEVER.)

he may have said something which / without him knowing or intending it / created grave offence /

(He shrugs.)

n'est-ce pas? /

(He laughs lightly.)

FEVER: Yes /

(He looks at the ground.)

I may even have deserved it /

(They watch him.)

for all I know /

(They drift on, then FORJAX calls back.)

FORJAX: It is so pretty here / I am reluctant to go back to town /

(FEVER remains in a posture of obeisance. FORJAX laughs tantalizingly.)

I <u>may</u> <u>not</u> go /

(Offstage now, THOMA giggles at her son's provocation.)

I <u>may</u> <u>not</u> / I <u>may</u> <u>not</u> /

(Their sounds fade. FEVER is alone. He sits in the chair, thoughtfully. He is about to rise to resume his labours when a faint cry reaches him on the wind. He stops, in mid-move. It is not repeated. He goes out.)

12

THOMA enters, uncharacteristically dressed in black. She occupies the chair. The sound of tools clattering precedes the appearance of FEVER, bearing an armful of long-handled implements in need of repair. He regards THOMA, who is mischievous. FEVER lets fall the tools, which clatter, and reaches into his apron for pincers. He applies them to the haft of a hoe.

THOMA: You look ridiculous /

> *(He hears but ignores this.)*

> always I think / seeing you with tools / boots / brushes / all things menial / he looks ridiculous /

> *(He watches her. Time passes.)*

> not really / I just / I hate to see you /

> *(She shrugs.)*

> <u>handling</u> <u>things</u> /

> *(She shifts.)*

> when you should be <u>handling</u> <u>me</u> /

> *(She laughs lightly. FEVER is suspicious. THOMA bounces a foot.)*

> I'm in mourning /

> *(She giggles. The distant cry reaches FEVER, but not THOMA.)*

FEVER: Mourning for whom / my lady? /

THOMA: *(Swiftly, cruelly.)* Don't my lady me /

> *(FEVER frowns, repudiating her.)*

> silly /

> *(They gaze.)*

> silly when you /

(She giggles.)

do what you do with me /

(She hurries on at once.)

mourning my marriage / obviously /

(FEVER hears the cry again. It divides his attention.)

darling /

(Her strange smile is transformed by pain.)

I'm 70 / I'm 70 /

(She stands and sits again. She does the same again. She laughs.)

I said / in dead of night this was / I said / 'I must have Fever / say no if you want to / if it's no it's no' / 'it's no' / he said /

(She watches FEVER for a long time.)

then he had me / oh /

(She bites her lip.)

how he /

FEVER: *(Desperately.)* I can't know this /

THOMA: How he /

FEVER: *(Definitely.)* I can't / I said /

THOMA: *(Undeterred.)* Had me I will describe to you another time /

(FEVER is restless with the contradiction of his situation, but hearing the cry again, stops. THOMA proceeds.)

and then / I knew this / I predicted it / hardly a day went by / he said /

(She shakes her head, laughing lightly.)

'I can't stop thinking of it' /

(She throws back her head and inhales deeply.)

'what?' / I said / disingenuously / 'what is it you can't stop thinking of?' /

(She is wan.)

'you know damned well' / he said /

(She shifts nervously.)

looking at me / looking in me / looking <u>at</u> <u>me</u> <u>and</u> <u>in</u> <u>me</u> /

(Her smile is pained.)

'not only <u>may</u> you / do whatever it is you want to do with him / but I <u>insist</u> you do it' /

(She fixes FEVER with her hardest gaze.)

my lord my husband said /

(FEVER is grim-faced.)

'did I marry you / a woman of 70 / for peace / possession / and propriety?' /

(She draws herself together.)

so / your having me is perfectly compatible with your servitude / and if it ever was /

(She smiles stiffly.)

it is no longer <u>theft</u> /

(She appeals to FEVER.)

take me somewhere / his tolerance for my iniquity does not extend to yielding us his bed /

(She is nervous, wild.)

<u>it</u> <u>might</u> <u>do</u> <u>yet</u> /

(She cuts off her humour, biting her lip. FEVER is aroused as ever by THOMA, whilst knowing something is compromised.)

FEVER: Obviously he'll /

(He is hesitant.)

inevitably he'll / expect you to describe what /

(He is alarmed for her.)

he might beat you / Thoma /

(She eliminates this anxiety with two words.)

THOMA: He won't /

FEVER: All right / but he'll /

THOMA: Yes /

(Through their profound look, the distant cry, now audible to neither of them.)

and I'll say / 'Fever's an old man / so it wasn't much' / which might comfort him /

(She is subtle as ever.)

comfort / but not arouse / and probably / it's hard to know with men / arousal is what he requires /

(She fidgets.)

my husband thinks you are the perfect lord /

(She plucks her garment nervously.)

FEVER: So does everyone /

THOMA: Yes /

FEVER: I can't think why /

(She thinks him disingenuous.)

THOMA: Because you are the perfect serf / obviously /

(She watches. She stands.)

now take me somewhere /

(The cry is heard, louder. EGYPT races by, calling to them.)

EGYPT: <u>They</u> <u>hurt</u> <u>the</u> <u>child</u> /

(He is gone. FEVER is distracted, and throwing aside the tool he has been holding all the time, goes to follow the youth. THOMA is absolute.)

THOMA: <u>Take me</u> / <u>I said</u> /

(Her command stops FEVER dead. He looks at THOMA.)

FEVER: The girl's /

(He sees the extent of THOMA'S determination. He disciplines himself.)

so what if the girl's /

(He studies her also.)

whatever it is the girl's /

THOMA: You're a serf /

FEVER: I am a serf / and what my lady says is /

(He creates a shape with his hands.)

law to a serf /

(He is deep in thought.)

and more than law / it's /

(He finds his word.)

excellence to me /

(He watches her.)

who loves serf /

(And wills himself.)

<u>dom</u> /

(THOMA'S gaze is terrible and wonderful. Taking the initiative, she strides out. FEVER waits, a contrived few seconds, then follows.)

13

BLEW enters. She is thoughtful, as if temper has gone out of her.

BLEW: Why would anyone /

(The question stands on its own, as if it were universal.)

why /

(FEVER enters, and sits. He crosses one leg over the other.)

why / Fever / why /

(He is silent. BLEW exclaims.)

and I hate <u>why</u> / always I find myself /

(She ponders, wanly.)

<u>stuck in why</u> /

(She is severe.)

but <u>why</u> /

(FEVER remains silent. BLEW aches and cannot release herself from her torment.)

a child with no / a /

(She shrugs.)

child with no /

FEVER: She liked me /

(This remark stops BLEW, who stares at FEVER.)

if there's any <u>why</u> at all /

(BLEW gawps.)

that might be <u>why</u> /

(She cannot respond.)

on the other hand / I did not much like her / her
determination to discover virtue in /

(He shrugs.)

everyone and everything / was not to my taste / still /

(Her frown stops FEVER. BLEW fathoms his meaning.)

BLEW: So this / this child / this inoffensive child / was
thrashed nearly to death /

(BLEW cannot credit FEVER'S logic.)

in order to spite you /

(FEVER is not mocked.)

FEVER: I / without intending to /

(He smiles thinly.)

we know this / don't we / Blew /

(He narrows his eyes.)

<u>create</u> problems /

(BLEW might bawl at him, but withholds. She waits.)

Or it's worse than that /

BLEW: *(Deeply cold.)* In what way could it be / <u>worse</u>? /

(FEVER'S reply comes from the depths of his solitude.)

FEVER: Blew / your heirs / if they inherit the indignation and
the vehemence of you / will rule the world / with their
questions / and their answers to the questions / and the
questions which arise / inexorably / from their answers /

(He nods faintly.)

to the questions /

(He controls his rage.)

and they / like you / will never know /

(He shrugs.)

and cannot know / cannot / <u>cannot</u> <u>know</u> /

(He is cold as her now.)

what cannot be a question /

(He stands at last.)

it is not preposterous / as your mean and twisted face exclaims / this child was beaten half to death / not to injure <u>her</u> / but to injure <u>me</u> /

(He frightens her.)

not preposterous / nor /

(He swallows.)

nor any more preposterous / to say it is a sign /

(BLEW senses FEVER is mad.)

BLEW: A sign? /

(He knows her contempt.)

FEVER: <u>A</u> <u>sign</u> /

(She looks cruelly.)

BLEW: The beating of her / a harmless child /

FEVER: And me / the beating of me /

BLEW: *(Conceding.)* And the beating of you /

FEVER: Who is no less harmless /

(She might argue this, but is content to pass it over.)

BLEW: Is a sign / is it / according to you? /

(He is patient.)

a sign of what? /

(FEVER does not know. The argument might cease, but FEVER, shaking his head ruefully, must persist.)

FEVER: Blew /

(He regrets persisting already.)

I say it's a sign / and you /

(He bites his lip.)

you can't help it /

(He frowns cruelly at her.)

must make a <u>question</u> of the <u>sign</u> /

(If BLEW'S madness is self-evident to FEVER, the reverse is also true. BLEW waits, not conceding the silence to him, then departs. FEVER stays stock-still, eyes on the ground.)

14

A pair of encrusted boots is flung in. They land near FEVER. A short time passes. RIBBONS enters. He studies FEVER, who lets a certain time elapse before gathering the boots.

FEVER: Everything wearies me but work / my lord /

(RIBBONS is silently amused.)

RIBBONS: Is that so / Fever? /

(His smile is awkward.)

my lady Thoma might be sad to learn this /

(He shrugs.)

though some call love labour / I don't know /

(FEVER wants no more argument today. He goes to leave.)

FEVER: I'll clean these now / my lord /

(RIBBONS concedes with a slight tilt of his head. As FEVER departs RIBBONS calls.)

RIBBONS: What's wrong here / Fever? /

(FEVER stops.)

you're clever / you must know /

(FEVER is reluctant.)

a serf / whilst steeped in ignorance /

(He laughs, ironically.)

still / if not through his intelligence / through his calloused fingers / might discern the crisis / and its /

(He hesitates.)

<u>resolution</u> /

(He is able to utter the words.)

I appeal to you /

FEVER: My lord need never /

RIBBONS: No /

FEVER: <u>Appeal</u> /

RIBBONS: *(Icily.)* Of course not / no /

FEVER: For things he is / in any case / entitled to /

RIBBONS: Yes / yes / but you see /

(He stops. He walks, thoughtfully, in a circular movement, and stops.)

what spins or crawls through a serf's brain is not his master's property / nor need a serf explain a fraction of his thought to any man /

(FEVER is wary.)

you are not a serf / Fever / you act your servitude / and like a no-good actor / you exaggerate the role /

(He shudders irritably.)

you make more onerous than they already are the obligations of /

(He rants now.)

you corrupt me with your /

(He cannot proceed. FEVER is still, his eyes on the ground. RIBBONS recollects his dignity.)

the old woman / Blew / someone tried to drown her /

FEVER: I heard /

(RIBBONS is uncritical.)

RIBBONS: It was you /

(FEVER is shaken by the charge.)

FEVER: My lord is /

(He struggles.)

in this instance /

RIBBONS: *(Warning FEVER.)* Serfdom /

(FEVER fails to grasp RIBBONS'S sarcasm.)

FEVER: I regret to say /

RIBBONS: *(Gravely.)* Serfdom / Fever /

(They look deeply.)

serfdom means the serf / that's you / agrees with
everything the lord / that's me / cares to propose /

(FEVER senses the mischief in his master.)

if I declare you guilty / then you must be /

(FEVER knows the logic of his own position.)

FEVER: Yes /

*(RIBBONS studies the ashlar expression on FEVER'S face, as if he
might enter it. Then he laughs, authentically.)*

RIBBONS: Of course you didn't do it /

(He throws up his hands.)

and anyway / if you were accused of this / or any
misdemeanour / what would our lady Thoma say? /

(He bites his lip, studying FEVER as closely as ever.)

<u>say?</u> / <u>say?</u> / she'd shout the roof off /

(He enjoys his parody.)

'hang <u>my</u> <u>serf</u> / <u>you</u> <u>may</u> <u>not</u> / <u>let</u> <u>him</u> <u>drown</u> <u>who</u> <u>he</u> <u>wants</u>
to' /

(He laughs again, then is grave.)

what is happening / Fever / to the estate? /

FEVER: My lord / I do not know /

(RIBBONS cannot be satisfied with this.)

RIBBONS: Not <u>know</u> / no / to say 'I know' /

(He closes his eyes.)

a reckless provocation /

(FORJAX enters idly, and takes the chair. He smiles at FEVER.)

FORJAX: I didn't go /

(RIBBONS scarcely reveals his irritation with FORJAX.)

RIBBONS: It's God who <u>knows</u> / we only <u>feel</u> / but the feelings / on rare occasions / coincide with the facts / so /

(He indicates FEVER should utter something. FEVER is slow to respond.)

FORJAX: <u>Black</u> <u>is</u> <u>not</u> <u>her</u> <u>colour</u> /

(RIBBONS is visibly irritated. FORJAX is unintimidated.)

is it? /

(RIBBONS restrains himself.)

her colour? /

(FORJAX bounces his foot, gazing at the ground.)

FEVER: If I were to enter my lord's place / and he /

(He affects modesty.)

grotesque speculation /

(He looks at the ground also.)

were enslaved to me /

FORJAX: *(Ignoring FEVER.)* With her skin / her so-white skin / she must wear white /

(FEVER is patient.)

this I discerned at an early age / and if anything / it is more true today /

(He boldly looks at RIBBONS.)

the fact her hair is white confirms my infantile perception that <u>white</u> <u>becomes</u> <u>white</u> /

(RIBBONS is cold with contempt, whereas FORJAX smiles. He concedes to FEVER.)

FEVER: If authority were shifted / broken / or abolished in its entirety /

(RIBBONS heeds acutely.)

nothing could alter / that is my <u>knowing</u> / my lord /

(FORJAX heeds also.)

my <u>feeling</u> / is that reason / argument / even philosophy / are sickly self-indulgences / and that everything is only / or precisely / what it has to be /

(RIBBONS looks sympathetically to FEVER, who is, rashly perhaps, emboldened to confess.)

I cannot tell you how much more difficult my slavery has been for me that you are not a worthless human being /

(He aches with his contradictions.)

I should have much preferred it if you were /

(Little of this is understood by RIBBONS, who might enquire further but is interrupted by FORJAX, grinning.)

FORJAX: Try me /

(He exclaims.)

I'm worthless /

(He sees his mother, and stands to greet her.)

aren't I / worthless / mother? /

(THOMA looks at her son dully, then at her husband.)

THOMA: The old woman's died /

(No one reacts immediately.)

the cantankerous old woman who was half-drowned /

(She is objective.)

is dead /

(She turns to FORJAX.)

<u>of</u> <u>course</u> <u>you</u> <u>are</u> <u>not</u> <u>worthless</u> /

(Her rebuke is stinging, but FORJAX is oddly hard in his reply.)

FORJAX: I am / and you look ridiculous in black /

(He goes to leave as RIBBONS, seething, issues a threat.)

RIBBONS: You may not /

(His fists clench.)

to my lady your mother / you may not /

(His head twists in his anger.)

in my presence / may not /

(And again turns.)

<u>may</u> <u>not</u> /

(FORJAX waits.)

<u>may</u> <u>not</u> /

(THOMA observes her son. With the slightest tilt of his head to RIBBONS, FORJAX leaves. RIBBONS takes a breath.)

FEVER: What Blew did / her obligations / I'll add to my own /

THOMA: That's silly /

FEVER: She did a lot less than others /

THOMA: Silly / I said /

FEVER: Whereas she was strict /

(RIBBONS observes the lovers curiously.)

it was the minimum she was strict about /

THOMA: *(Bawling at FEVER.)* What is the matter with you /
you're 70 /

(She glares. She senses the gaze of her husband.)

1 / 2 / what are you /

(She turns to RIBBONS.)

tell him he can't / say he cannot do two people's work /

RIBBONS: *(Complacently.)* Obviously he cannot do two people's work /

FEVER: *(Scrupulously.)* My lord will find it difficult to recruit a substitute for Blew / the labourers are leaving / in the dead of night / usually / I hear their creaking handcarts /

(He grimly smiles.)

a fatuous consumption of their energy since everywhere things are the same /

THOMA: This they will see / presumably /

FEVER: Presumably /

THOMA: In which case / they will turn around /

FEVER: I daresay /

THOMA: And come back here /

FEVER: That would be my preference / certainly /

THOMA: Given that my lord is generous to his tenants /

FEVER: And my lady / so is she /

(Their mutual gaze, semi-antagonistic, intrigues RIBBONS, who himself gazes on their gaze.)

RIBBONS: A <u>cliché</u> /

(He admits.)

not <u>yet</u> a cliché / a cliché in its infancy /

(He proposes.)

'when times are bad / speak with donkeys' /

175

(He waits for their reaction. THOMA watches RIBBONS. FEVER senses an obligation to respond.)

FEVER: Of all my lord's clichés / this must rank among the most opaque /

THOMA: Opaque / why /

FEVER: Given that /

THOMA: What's opaque about it? /

FEVER: It does not imply /

THOMA: *(Irritably.)* It doesn't imply anything /

(She regrets her tetchiness.)

I'm tired / I'm tired / I might lie down / no / I can't / I can't start lying down whenever I / I'll end up bed-ridden /

(She alters instantly.)

in what way opaque? / I'll sit /

(She goes to the chair.)

sit / not lie /

(She sprawls.)

FEVER: My lord's cliché does not imply / as you might expect it to / that in bad times donkeys acquire the gift of speech / that we are led astray by donkeys / indeed / if I am not mistaken / it proposes the opposite / that /

(He is hesitant.)

in bad times we may as well speak with donkeys / for all the good speech does /

(RIBBONS is bemused.)

THOMA: All right / that's what it means /

(She jumps up.)

I'm not tired / I'm /

(She seems to become fixed. A great sigh comes from her, followed by a profound sobbing. RIBBONS, for a fraction of a second, might yield his place to FEVER, then resuming his role as husband, goes to comfort THOMA. She recoils.)

I can't fuck now / I can't fuck now / I can't fuck / I can't fuck /

(UNBORN, appearing modestly at the edge of things, inhibits further argument. THOMA, altered in an instant, smiles and goes to her.)

15

THOMA: You are recovered / you are completely recovered / we were so /

(She looks to RIBBONS.)

weren't we / so afraid /

UNBORN: Thank you /

THOMA: You'd be lamed / or /

UNBORN: Thank you /

THOMA: Something horrible we /

(She falters.)

UNBORN: For the jellies / and the / the /

(Now she falters.)

everything you sent /

(She curtsies very slightly.)

my lady /

(THOMA is silent, speechless. She walks away. RIBBONS delays a while longer.)

RIBBONS: Rest /

(He nods, and nods.)

as long as you need /

(UNBORN repeats her curtsy. RIBBONS goes off in the direction of his wife. UNBORN waits before speaking to FEVER.)

UNBORN: The funeral was short / the priest said Blew was good / her husband wondered why you weren't there /

(FEVER does not reply.)

I wondered /

(Still he is silent.)

you did not care for Blew / but /

FEVER: There's the reason /

(UNBORN shrugs.)

UNBORN: That's so like you / to be so scrupulous with your own feelings to attend a funeral even / poses a dilemma /

(She twists in her anxiety.)

she said you did it /

(FEVER is not shocked, but frowns.)

Blew /

(He is still.)

she didn't see who did it / but it was you /

(UNBORN bites her lip. FEVER goes to the tools, still lying about the place, and tests one or two before selecting a spade.)

FEVER: Tell Egypt / leave off ditching /

UNBORN: He's not ditching /

FEVER: What is he doing? /

UNBORN: The barn stair /

FEVER: Tell him leave that off / and if you're fit / the three of us can /

UNBORN: *(Desperately.)* Did you / Fever / did you half-drown Blew? /

(FEVER resents her interrogation, but wants it ended.)

FEVER: You are not my lord / Unborn / nor are you my lady / and I will never confirm nor deny a thing to you /

(She gazes boldly.)

I will however state what you already ought to know / by looking or listening /

(He is grave.)

I do nothing unless I am ordered to /

(He is about to set off, but UNBORN is not daunted, but coy.)

UNBORN: Perhaps you were /

(FEVER stops.)

ordered to? /

(FEVER'S contempt is barely concealed by his patience.)

FEVER: And why would my lord Ribbons / who is so short of labour / command me to inflict a cruel and pointless injury on his own /

UNBORN: Lord Ribbons might not /

FEVER: His own /

UNBORN: Lord Ribbons might not / no /

(FEVER senses the uncanny in UNBORN as never before.)

even so / you might be ordered /

(FEVER intensifies his patience into a weapon.)

FEVER: By whom? /

(UNBORN smiles disconcertingly.)

by whom ordered? /

(She simply smiles. FEVER is provoked.)

as everybody knows / more than a dozen have been hurt round here /

(His patience falters.)

a clerk / a soldier recently /

UNBORN: *(Assuming an ascendancy.)* Shh /

FEVER: *(Ill-tempered now.)* Do you think I go from one place to another /

UNBORN: Silly /

FEVER: Wounding and smothering and /

UNBORN: Silly / silly / no /

(FEVER bridles. He hates her lingering smile.)

there are many of you / and it's catching / like the plague /

(FEVER is grim.)

and as with any plague / you can't say / 'he's to blame for catching it' /

(She shrugs cheerfully.)

it's the devil / Fever / it's the devil orders you /

(She regards him, almost flirtatiously. FEVER must conclude things.)

FEVER: Find a spade / tell Egypt we are in the /

(He stops. He rebukes her.)

you are looking at me in a way I hate /

(She is unrepentant.)

I'll tell Egypt myself / you'll find us in the /

(He seethes.)

the smile on your /

(She alters nothing.)

the smile which is not smiling /

UNBORN: *(Abolishing it.)* Smack the smile then / smack it off my face /

(FEVER is yet more disturbed. He concludes things swiftly.)

FEVER: Rest longer / rest days / rest weeks /

(He goes out abruptly, passing her. UNBORN remains.)

16

A frantic cry precedes the appearance of RIBBONS.

RIBBONS: <u>Fever</u> /

(RIBBONS strides in.)

have you seen him /

(He calls again.)

<u>Fe</u> - <u>ver</u> /

(He commands UNBORN.)

fetch him here / say I need him / say drop everything /

(UNBORN seems too preoccupied to act. Before RIBBONS can insist, THOMA hurtles in, wild-eyed, her hands clenched.)

THOMA: <u>It's</u> <u>you</u> / <u>it's</u> <u>you</u> /

RIBBONS: <u>It</u> <u>was</u> <u>not</u> <u>me</u> /

(THOMA goes to attack her husband, who seizes her wrists.)

nothing is me / and you are /

(They spin around in their struggle.)

Thoma /

(She tears free and renews her attack.)

Thoma /

(Again he seizes her wrists and at the same time bawls at UNBORN.)

get Fever here /

(UNBORN seems bemused by the domestic contretemps, and only slowly retires, looking over her shoulder as RIBBONS fixes his wife, who screams.)

THOMA: Killer / killer /

RIBBONS: I'll slap you / I'll slap you /

THOMA: You hated him / you hated him / always you hated him /

(His grip causes her pain.)

ow / ow /

RIBBONS: I have never / ever /

THOMA: Ow / ow /

RIBBONS: Laid a finger / on your son /

(THOMA fixes her husband with an appalling stare.)

THOMA: I am a hundred /

(He does not free her. She wails.)

a hundred years old / let me go /

(RIBBONS gazes, distrusting her. At last he frees her hands. She sobs desperately. FEVER enters. RIBBONS looks at him, and departs. THOMA seems to hang from nothing. FEVER waits. She becomes strangely calm.)

My son /

(FEVER waits.)

did you notice this? / could hardly breathe /

(She emits a small laugh.)

the air <u>we</u> breathe / was poisonous to him /

(FEVER looks at the ground.)

so sensitive and /

(She shakes her head, grieving.)

so tender / was my son /

(FEVER waits.)

FEVER: Your husband did not murder him /

THOMA: *(Knowing this.)* No /

FEVER: Which is a shame / in some ways /

(THOMA dredges sarcasm from her depths.)

THOMA: A shame / is it / my husband did not murder my
son? /

(Her look on him is withering but FEVER is undeterred.)

FEVER: Yes / because he had a reason / compelling in my
opinion / to have done so /

(She watches him. He proceeds.)

my lord Ribbons is / and always was / infatuated with his
lady / and must possess the whole of her /

(He is pointed.)

even her infidelities he must own /

(THOMA scowls.)

but <u>this</u> / this / dark estate of her maternity / where the child commands her wardrobe / and the colour of her clothes /

THOMA: *(Angrily.)* He did not /

FEVER: <u>My</u> <u>lord</u> <u>is</u> <u>lost</u> <u>in</u> <u>there</u> /

THOMA: <u>Command</u> <u>my</u> <u>wardrobe</u> /

(They look fiercely into one another.)

FEVER: *(Coolly.)* And he was right / white becomes my lady /

(THOMA seethes.)

THOMA: You also /

FEVER: As black does / God knows /

THOMA: You also hated him /

(FEVER does not deny this.)

hated my /

(She is determined to be truthful.)

<u>uncommon</u> / son /

(She might collapse. Her mouth is so tightly closed no words can escape it. She must however, announce something, at last.)

I washed him /

(FEVER loves THOMA but keeps his distance.)

and if I was 70 when I began / I was 100 by the time that it was done /

(He waits.)

and at 100 /

(She is cruel and deliberate.)

no one /

(She is narrow-eyed.)

surely /

(FEVER guesses her drift.)

do they /

(And is correct.)

fucks? /

(FEVER does not dispute his punishment, and lowers his head. THOMA bites her lip, gazing on his submission for a long while. Then she surges out. Immediately she returns, and flings herself into his arms, breathless, mad.)

I won't cry you / I won't cry you / I'll cry my boy /

(THOMA weeps and laughs as FEVER encloses her in his arms, kissing and soothing her.)

I'll cry my boy / not you /

(FEVER lifts her and carries her out. Her uncanny sounds float in.)

17

EGYPT, failing to avoid UNBORN, is persecuted by her.

UNBORN: You've not been killed / have you? /

    (EGYPT keeps withdrawing.)

    have you / Egypt /

    (He faces her.)

    been killed? /

EGYPT: Killed / no /

UNBORN: No / nor beaten either /

    (He gawps. He lifts his hands.)

even Fever has been beaten / and Fever's one of them /

EGYPT: You sound like Blew /

UNBORN: Yes / someone must be Blew / if there's no more Blew /

(UNBORN glares. EGYPT is at bay.)

fetch a pole / I'll hit you /

EGYPT: I don't want to be hit /

UNBORN: You've got to be hit /

(EGYPT squirms.)

and bruised /

(He winces.)

quite badly bruised /

EGYPT: *(Resuming his retreat.)* I'm wanted at the house /

UNBORN: Be wise / Egypt / be wise / people see /

(EGYPT is in two minds.)

EGYPT: See what? /

UNBORN: That you're unhurt / silly /

(EGYPT looks uncomfortable.)

two minutes / and I promise not to hit your head /

(He frowns.)

it's /

(She shrugs in irritation.)

oh / it's /

(She lifts her hands.)

maddening / how people will not be helped /

(She sniffs.)

maddening /

(And shakes her head.)

maddening /

(RIBBONS enters. He appears vague, hardly observing the serfs, who bow swiftly.)

EGYPT: On my way / my lord /

(RIBBONS looks up, puzzled. EGYPT sets off. UNBORN curtsies in an offhand way.)

UNBORN: So sorry / my lord / I speak for everyone / so sorry for my lady's son /

(RIBBONS lifts his gaze and seems to study UNBORN.)

and my lady Thoma / for her too /

(They look.)

to be fucked by Fever helps no one /

(RIBBONS simply looks.)

no wonder she screams /

(UNBORN recklessly invents.)

I did / oh / I screamed / probably you heard me /

(She laughs in her way.)

and I'm barely 20 /

(She goes to the chair.)

at 71 /

(She sits, looks boldly at RIBBONS.)

she's beyond help / surely / my lady? /

(They sustain a cool regard.)

the nuns took in mad women / I could make enquiries /
though one of them has been attacked / they might not be
so charitable / as they were formerly /

*(RIBBONS cuts her off with a flick of his hand. UNBORN simply
looks back. At last he speaks.)*

RIBBONS: I'm not sorry /

*(UNBORN waits for an elaboration which does not come. She
presumes.)*

UNBORN: He was a fool / my lady's son /

RIBBONS: *(Clarifying.)* Not sorry my wife is mad /

(UNBORN waits.)

to love / what is it / to love? /

(She shrugs.)

let her rave /

(He is thoughtful, calm.)

go naked where she shouldn't /

(He is moved by his passion.)

and piss the flower beds in full view of / etcetera /

(He challenges UNBORN, nearly angry.)

you love / you love all /

(She nods, faintly wary.)

all / all /

UNBORN: Yes /

RIBBONS: And the more the all is / the more you love the all /
is that true for you / Fever? /

*(UNBORN has not discerned FEVER'S arrival behind her. He is
discreet as ever.)*

FEVER: My lord's passion for his lady is / if not yet legendary / surely destined to become so /

RIBBONS: That isn't what I asked /

(UNBORN emits a shrill laugh.)

I asked if you still have my lady Thoma / madness notwithstanding /

(FEVER is constrained by UNBORN, as RIBBONS knows.)

say / Fever / say /

(He discreetly declines. RIBBONS waits some time.)

when my lady dies / you will bury me beside her /

FEVER: Yes / my lord /

RIBBONS: Alive /

FEVER: Yes / my lord /

RIBBONS: That's proper /

FEVER: Yes / my lord /

RIBBONS: That I / the lover of my wife / am /

(UNBORN cannot contain her incredulity and laughs shrilly. She bites her lip. RIBBONS waits, then proceeds.)

while you fling cold clay on my naked back /

(UNBORN looks to FEVER, expecting a retort which does not come. RIBBONS makes to go.)

and this is imminent / oh / imminent / if my lady does not catch her death wandering and muttering on these freezing nights / she'll be killed by the killers /

(He looks severely at FEVER.)

preserve yourself / Fever /

FEVER: I'll try / my lord / if only to be sure a pair of hands remains to /

(FEVER hesitates under RIBBONS'S scrutiny.)

dig / the / grave /

(Something rash overflows FEVER'S habitual manner.)

in which my lord will be /

(He dares on.)

frantically /

(And on.)

squirming / on the cold corpse of his wife /

(RIBBONS receives this without complaint. UNBORN is struck silent. RIBBONS is suddenly pitiful and desperate.)

RIBBONS: And will that be the end of it / do you think /

(FEVER has no answer. RIBBONS ponders.)

as I lie suffocating in the clay / or chalk /

(He enquires.)

what is it here? /

FEVER: My lord / it's chalk /

RIBBONS: And you walk away / and fling aside the filthy spade / and tired from your exertions / sprawl in a seat / and drink / and stare / and scratch an itch / beneath the moon /

(He looks into FEVER.)

is that the end of it / or does she / scarcely a bone / remain a thought / inside my thought /

(FEVER has nothing to offer him.)

thought having /

(He shrugs.)

a place somewhere / no matter that the brain that hatched it / sank into the /

(He stops. He is irritated with himself.)

clay / did you say? /

FEVER: *(Patiently.)* Chalk /

(RIBBONS is pained. His body aches.)

RIBBONS: Nothingness / intolerable / don't you think? /

(For a moment, FEVER deems silence most appropriate, but then must utter.)

FEVER: On the contrary / it is the thing I most look forward to /

(RIBBONS nods. He does not care to challenge FEVER. He walks slowly away, stops, lifts a finger and points.)

RIBBONS: <u>Lord</u> /

(He laughs mildly.)

<u>lord</u> /

(FEVER looks down.)

didn't I always say so? /

(He continues out, but scarcely has he departed, but UNBORN, dragging a small knife, from her clothes, goes to stab FEVER. FEVER seizes her wrist with one hand and smacks her face with the other. She cries out and drops the blade. FEVER overcomes the desire to kill UNBORN, instead twisting her to her knees.)

18

FEVER: All things /

(She exclaims.)

all things /

(She writhes.)

<u>point</u> /

(She twists. He bends her yet more cruelly.)

<u>to</u> <u>me</u> /

(UNBORN cries out more urgently.)

and still I /

(FEVER makes a knot of UNBORN'S body. She is beyond protest.)

still I /

(He lets go of her.)

decline to be / what the world implores me to be /

(She is a motionless heap.)

and it becomes harder obviously / with the madness of the lords / harder to <u>serve</u> /

(He meditates.)

but why? /

(And frowns in thought.)

is it not a deeper servitude / a deeper and more pure servitude / one I surely should aspire to / when my very soul is stung by everything I am called upon to do / the field / the fuck / the shoe? /

(He kicks the fallen UNBORN.)

what do you think? /

(At last UNBORN emits a sob. FEVER gazes down on her indifferently. EGYPT enters, an arm in a sling, his head in a bandage.)

isn't there something /

(He observes EGYPT'S condition and ignores it.)

something / <u>doglike</u> / <u>horselike</u> / in this predisposition to refuse a thing you dread? /

(He shrugs.)

I have seen a horse shy from a too-high fence /

(He smiles cruelly.)

let's not dignify it / describing this as human and so on / let's not applaud ourselves / let's not / let's not /

(He turns to go, but looks back. His gaze includes EGYPT'S injuries.)

is there anybody left to dig? /

(EGYPT shakes his head stupidly.)

then I must do the digging /

(He turns. EGYPT wails.)

EGYPT: You can't / you can't / Fever / leave us on our own like this /

(He bursts into tears.)

you can't /

(He wails.)

you <u>can't</u> /

(Tears pour down his face. FEVER is not without pity, and seems in two minds. THOMA passes through, in white, and a white sunhat.)

THOMA: He prefers it /

(She laughs lightly.)

don't you / prefer to be the one who <u>might</u> / the one who <u>could</u> /

(She looks at him.)

but <u>never</u> <u>will</u> /

(Rather than dispute this, FEVER bows to THOMA, who stops on her way out.)

you're pale /

(He says nothing.)

all weathers you are out / and still you're pale /

(She goes. EGYPT sniffs. FEVER takes EGYPT by the shoulder, almost affectionately.)

FEVER: When you <u>serve</u> / oh / how obtuse of me it was not to understand this / you must be seen to serve reluctantly / however small the signs / in the eyes / or in the lips / or the master gets no satisfaction from his domination /

(He smiles oddly.)

now that <u>is</u> human /

(He shakes EGYPT slightly in his pleasure.)

<u>that</u> you would not find in horse / or dog /

(He also sniffs.)

I think /

(And laughs.)

I <u>think</u> /

(He nods, looking at EGYPT.)

in some ways / therefore / I am a much worse serf than you / whilst being in all ways better /

(He is grave, at once, as if he sensed a calamity. He turns abruptly, and strains his hearing, turning his head to catch a remote sound.

Seeing him off-guard, UNBORN goes to snatch the knife off the ground, but again FEVER is quicker and knocks her aside. She stumbles and yells.)

shut <u>up</u> / shut <u>up</u> /

(She obeys, in dread of him. FEVER walks a pace or two, listening. EGYPT is a picture of dumb confusion. Something assures FEVER what he hears is what he presumes it to be. He seems depleted. He turns back into the scene. UNBORN scowls.)

all right /

(The knife lies between them.)

all right /

(EGYPT is open-mouthed at the prospect of a savage act. FEVER is persistent.)

all right /

(UNBORN cannot.)

all right /

(She lifts her hands to her ears.)

all right /

19

UNBORN fails to act and FEVER'S words hurt her. She tears out. He takes the chair. He disposes himself. EGYPT stands adjacent to the chair like a courtier. As FEVER expects, THOMA enters, hatless, her clothing soiled. She stands before him. He observes her. She pulls blades of grass off her dress. Time passes.

FEVER: *(At last.)* I said all right /

(She plucks.)

all right / I said / by all right I meant /

(He stops.)

I meant a great deal / but the great deal I meant was perfectly contained in those two syllables /

(He regards THOMA.)

she failed /

THOMA: We all do /

FEVER: Yes /

THOMA: We all fail you /

FEVER: Yes /

THOMA: We are so / so /

(She giggles faintly.)

whereas you / you are /

FEVER: *(Irritably.)* I am / my lady / yes /

(THOMA strokes her neck, lovingly. She is suddenly inspired.)

THOMA: Cliché /

(She waits, for effect.)

'sad is the bride / and the widow / she /

(She stops.)

she' /

(She seems deflated.)

finish it for me / darling / I'm not very good at these /

(FEVER does not supply her.)

these /

(She trails off.)

FEVER: Where is he / your lord your husband /

(THOMA bites her hand, gazing at FEVER, who swiftly laughs.)

I say where / as if there <u>was</u> somewhere / he might be everywhere / is he? / <u>everywhere</u> / and /

(She looks.)

<u>in</u> <u>parts?</u> /

EGYPT: *(A cry.)* They do that /

FEVER: They do /

EGYPT: Heads in one place /

FEVER: Yes /

EGYPT: Legs /

(He draws in his breath.)

could be anywhere / the legs /

(He sniffs.)

I was lucky /

(He looks at FEVER.)

so were you /

FEVER: *(Whose gaze remains on THOMA.)* Not lucky / no / how often do I need remind you / you are a serf /

(EGYPT is silenced.)

they would not stoop to butcher <u>you</u> /

(He waits.)

as for me /

(He waits longer. He stands abruptly.)

<u>I</u> <u>can</u> <u>finish</u> <u>it</u> /

(He resurrects the cliché.)

'Sad is the bride / and the widow /

(He states it emphatically.)

glad / is / she' /

(THOMA'S gaze is bemused, uncritical.)

of course / that's not a cliché / the cliché / first and foremost / needs to be sentimental / it must reconcile us to the sheer ugliness of things /

(He laughs, briefly.)

you need to wash your face /

(THOMA ignores this.)

the clichés we have created here /

EGYPT: *(Puzzled.)* Why are widows glad / Fever? /

FEVER: Resonate with /

EGYPT: They cry / don't they? /

FEVER: Nobody /

EGYPT: My mum / when my dad died / you should have seen my mum /

FEVER: I'll wash it /

EGYPT: She was / oh / they crying of my mum /

FEVER: I'll wash your face /

(FEVER walks away, looks back. THOMA follows.)

EGYPT: She wasn't glad /

(He observes their departure. The more he thinks, the more indignant he becomes.)

not at all glad / Fever /

(He scowls.)

Blew said /

(He recalls.)

Fever's <u>waiting</u> / only <u>waiting</u> / and god help you when he /

(He calls.)

she got you / did Blew /

(There is no response. He sniffs. The silence makes him afraid. He resumes his servility. He calls.)

shall I weed the flower-beds? /

(Nothing comes back.)

with one arm / I can hoe a bit /

(The land is empty, and he feels its emptiness. He calls out.)

<u>take</u> <u>over</u> /

(He looks about him. He shouts.)

<u>take</u> <u>over</u> /

(There is nothing from FEVER.)

who cares if you / what you /

(He writhes.)

how you /

(His fear masters him.)

fuck Blew / someone has to / when things are /

(His eyes swivel.)

and if you're mental / a little bit /

(His laugh is false.)

or <u>very</u> <u>mental</u> / still / who isn't / from time to time /

(And looks again around him.)

mental / I say / I say /

(He smiles grimly.)

so lord Fever's mental / but the walls are whitewashed / and the roofs are tiled / and if a few /

(He is placid now.)

get what's coming to them /

(And without rage.)

good /

20

FEVER appears, discreetly. Sensing him, EGYPT turns.

FEVER: Boots? /

(EGYPT is puzzled.)

EGYPT: Boots? /

(He frowns.)

whose boots? /

FEVER: Yours /

EGYPT: My boots? /

FEVER: Your boots / yes / I'm cleaning them /

(EGYPT is thrown into confusion.)

EGYPT: But you're /

FEVER: Yes / I am /

(EGYPT struggles.)

a serf without a master / but to have no master does not extinguish the instincts of a /

(EGYPT senses a rebuke.)

a <u>proper</u> <u>serf</u> /

(And feels it.)

he merely seeks a substitute / so deeply is his soul
immersed in his condition /

(He alters swiftly.)

and you may not attend the funeral / of our lord Ribbons /

(EGYPT is suddenly inspired.)

EGYPT: <u>Cut</u> <u>to</u> /

(FEVER is patient.)

FEVER: Looking like you do /

EGYPT: <u>Ribbons</u> /

(The coincidence troubles him.)

<u>cut</u> <u>to</u> <u>ribbons</u> /

FEVER: *(Ignoring this.)* I have washed my lady Thoma / and
following a lengthy and / heated / argument /

EGYPT: I heard /

FEVER: You heard / as to whether she is / strictly speaking / a
widow / or a bride / decided /

(He smiles coldly.)

in conformity with that melancholy human desire to love
the future and to loathe the past /

(He waits.)

she will attend this funeral in <u>white</u> /

*(EGYPT'S face causes FEVER to laugh in an uncharacteristically
uncontrolled way.)*

EGYPT: *(Mocking.)* You're not cleaning my boots /

201

FEVER: Oh / but I am / I am /

EGYPT: Fever / no /

FEVER: Sit / sit /

EGYPT: *(Serious now.)* Fever / it offends me /

(FEVER is troubled by this. He seems to contemplate.)

FEVER: I will not clean the soles / or polish them /

(EGYPT shakes his head. FEVER is overshadowed by his dread.)

sit / or I will break your jaw /

(EGYPT is aghast.)

EGYPT: I'm only a boy /

FEVER: Mmm /

EGYPT: Only a boy / Fever / and the world is horrible /

(FEVER flings himself on EGYPT, who cries out as he is propelled into the chair and fixed there. His head hangs. He sobs. FEVER is calm and stands back. At last he takes brushes from his apron and kneeling, works on EGYPT'S encrusted boots. The sounds are complimentary, the crying, the brushing, an accompaniment to THOMA'S entrance. Sensing her, EGYPT turns his head to her. He cries more in his shame. THOMA passes through, twirling a parasol. FEVER is not distracted from the task in hand, but finishes it before rising swiftly to his feet.)

FEVER: Now / go with my lady Thoma /

(EGYPT rises to his feet.)

and stand by her /

(EGYPT nods.)

<u>by</u> means <u>near</u> /

(And nods again.)

not <u>close</u> /

(And again.)

be discreet /

(EGYPT prepares to go.)

old women / at the graveside / their hearts / their knees /
their wombs /

(EGYPT stares.)

desert-dry and fragile / but no one knows what tides still
flow in them /

(He smiles stiffly.)

them least of all / so /

(EGYPT waits.)

<u>stand</u> <u>by</u> <u>her</u> /

(FEVER loosens his apron.)

go now / I'm following /

(EGYPT goes to leave, stops.)

EGYPT: It's a good thing / in some ways / we only found the
head and hands /

(He shrugs.)

the whole of him / we never could have managed / could
we /

(He shrugs again.)

me being like this /

(He moves his arm in its sling.)

and you /

(He is delicate.)

<u>old</u> /

(FEVER says nothing.)

you'd think / although it's horrible /

(EGYPT pulls a face.)

somebody must have planned it all /

(EGYPT does not linger with the thought, but goes out. FEVER removes his apron and is about to proceed with things when he catches a glimpse of his own boots, not polished to his satisfaction. He raises a foot up to the chair and works swiftly with the apron as a cloth. He repeats the action with the other foot but this time remains in the awkward posture, quite still, apron to boot. Slowly, he straightens himself, and lets the apron fall to the floor. His foot remains raised to the chair, as if thought paralyzed him. UNBORN, in a form of mourning dress, hurries in.)

UNBORN: Box / she says /

(He ignores her.)

everybody's waiting /

(And ignores this also.)

<u>box</u> / <u>she</u> <u>says</u> /

(She is exasperated.)

FEVER: On our way /

(He instructs her to go with a jerk of his head. She is obedient and departs. FEVER at last removes his leg, but is still inhibited by a thought, which he articulates as a conversation.)

I said / 'do you know how terrible you are / the sight of you / the odour of your decay / women / children / recoil from you' / he said / 'I don't need a mirror to show me to myself / nor your frown / nor the fact you hold your nose / and the deeper my corruption the more I rejoice in it / because I made it / I made my pain / and when it becomes intolerable to me / I will beg you slit my throat / and when

you do / I will know / even that / that even / was my
decision / and mine alone' /

*(He seems wounded by this, and unable to resolve it, as several false
moves indicate. EGYPT hastens in.)*

<u>yes</u> /

*(EGYPT dares not quarrel, but conveys his message with a gesture of
his unbandaged hand.)*

on our way /

(EGYPT seems unconvinced.)

<u>on</u> <u>our</u> <u>way</u> /

*(EGYPT is intimidated and leaves, passing THOMA, who has followed
him down. She ignores his glance. She waits at the edge of the stage.
FEVER might collect the casket of RIBBONS, but is delayed by his
worry.)*

so /

(He lifts a finger.)

so the lord / <u>decides</u> /

*(He drifts out, and returns with a wooden box under his arm,
stoutly but crudely made. He stares at the ground, stopped by the
thought again.)*

or /

or /

<u>disdaining</u> decision /

(He looks up to see THOMA.)

yields decision to the world / a world which every instinct
of a lord confirms he must despise /

(THOMA looks critical.)

on our way /

THOMA: *(Coolly.)* Good /

    (She folds her parasol, and leans on it.)

    good because / waiting in a churchyard / posed around a hole which is / you know /

FEVER: I dug the hole /

THOMA: You dug it / scarcely the normal size of hole /

    (She rebukes him.)

    you begin to feel foolish /

FEVER: *(Conciliatory.)* Yes /

THOMA: You think / if I meet that woman's eyes /

FEVER: Yes /

THOMA: I'll laugh /

FEVER: And did you? /

THOMA: No / I came down here instead /

FEVER: That was wise /

    (They are silent. She seems to evaluate FEVER.)

THOMA: We fuck after /

    (He nods. She is suddenly volatile.)

    or <u>now</u> / or <u>now</u> /

    (She laughs girlishly.)

    not now / not now /

    (And exquisite sadness overcomes her.)

    we could now /

    (She is sensible.)

    best not now /

(And dismisses the idea.)

not now / no /

(And shakes her head.)

no /

(And seems resolved.)

<u>certainly</u> <u>not</u> <u>now</u> /

(THOMA is filled with a sense of the meaningless of things, and still leaning on her parasol, frowns. Her melancholy communicates itself to FEVER, still holding the small coffin. They separately regain their equilibrium. FEVER reveres her, as never before.)

go / I'll follow /

(FEVER heaves the box onto his shoulder. He takes a pace or two, then looks back.)

<u>go</u> / <u>go</u> /

(He has scarcely moved again before THOMA cries out.)

darling / I cannot / after this / cannot bury another / I cannot / so /

(She bites her lip. They are still.)

FEVER: I shan't be killed /

(FEVER'S confidence is not shared by THOMA.)

Dying I don't know about / but I shan't be killed / nor you either /

(He lightly laughs.)

notwithstanding I have heard it muttered here and there / 'if my lady Thoma got strangled / would that be cruel / or kind?' /

(She is bemused.)

as if you were a blind and lame dog / no /

(He is categorical.)

it's <u>over</u> /

(THOMA stares, and believes him.)

now / your husband's head is heavy /

(THOMA'S smile is ambiguous.)

the accumulated sediments of love / desire petrified / a thousand aspects of his lady's nakedness made stone /

(He frowns.)

it weighs a ton / so /

(Their gaze lingers. FEVER dissolves into a weary laugh, and sets off. THOMA watches his progress, as if intending to follow at a prescribed distance, but never does. Instead she goes to the chair and sits, spreading her legs wide and poking the ground with her parasol like a bored child. UNBORN hurries in. Nothing funereal attaches to her now.)

21

UNBORN: *(Joyous.)* I have a child /

(THOMA seems not to have heard, and moves her parasol about, gazing at the ground.)

call it <u>Future</u> / he said / because it is /

(THOMA ignores all.)

I thought / I know you / not long ago you cracked my head open /

(She waits for some response but THOMA scratches the ground, audibly and intently, as if she were engraving it. UNBORN waits, then spits her defiance.)

so what /

(And again.)

<u>so</u> <u>what</u> /

(She resumes an artificial gaiety.)

I'm not the only one / all the women who <u>could</u> <u>be</u> /

(She laughs unpleasantly.)

<u>were</u> /

(She bites her hand.)

and some who couldn't be / still <u>were</u> /

(She is vaguely delirious now.)

I said / tentatively / <u>tentatively</u> said / they can't all be called <u>Future</u> / surely? /

(She watches THOMA'S slow moves.)

oh yes / they said /

(She plucks her sleeve.)

it'll sort itself out / and in a way it's holy / I thought that / as they walked away / it's <u>holy</u> /

(She is in a state of despair and rage.)

doesn't God say /

(At last THOMA ceases and leans back in the chair, regarding UNBORN with detachment.)

<u>love</u> <u>your</u> <u>enemies?</u> /

(UNBORN'S faith collapses at once.)

it'll sort itself out /

(She heaves out a sob.)

it'll sort itself out /

(Her second sob is a cry to heaven. Her hands hang at her sides. THOMA returns to her task. FEVER enters. He observes the condition of UNBORN in silence. The sole sound is made by THOMA'S engraving the soil.)

FEVER: To make nothing / to add nothing / to alter nothing /

(He goes to UNBORN and sits at her feet.)

to leave the world as you found it /

(UNBORN sniffs.)

exquisite /

(He folds his hands over his knees.)

to deny even / the paltry act that makes a child /

(Hearing this, THOMA emits a short laugh.)

yes /

yes /

(She scrapes.)

no accident that we /

(He is bemused.)

our age and our sterility /

(He finds this only word again.)

exquisite /

UNBORN: *(Placing her faith in him.)* Fever /

(She struggles to speak it.)

they made us lie down in a row /

FEVER: I saw /

(She is not surprised.)

UNBORN: You saw /

(She need not continue, but must.)

you saw /

(She does not protest.)

harder than God you are / to see and not to act /

(She forms her resolution.)

I do not love my enemies /

(And affirms.)

I do not /

(She is uncannily radiant.)

and this future the killers put in me /

(THOMA ceases engraving the ground.)

won't come about /

(She surges away. None of this surprises FEVER, who remains still for some moments, but her accusations have provoked him, and he scrambles to his feet. An old man now, he staggers, whilst pointing an accusing finger at her retreating back. His arm struggles in the air. He articulates nothing. His arm sinks down.)

THOMA: Are you killing me today? /

(FEVER seems not to have heard this, still gazing away.)

was it today? / I've forgotten what we said /

(FEVER responds at last, still not regarding her.)

FEVER: If it's an order / my lady /

(THOMA laughs, genuinely. FEVER shares her humour, going to her now.)

if it is /

(He removes a hairbrush from his garments and meticulously attends to her.)

certainly / living under the <u>killers</u> /

(He plucks hairs out the brush.)

the killers who are not killers any more /

(He resumes.)

will pose problems for my lady / whose appetite for mischief has surely /

THOMA: *(Coolly.)* Shut up /

(He accedes, but not for long.)

FEVER: Diminished with /

THOMA: *(Bemused.)* Shut up /

(He brushes. He must go on.)

FEVER: And there is no chance / a woman so beautiful / so old / and wearing white /

(She does not arrest his thought.)

can be ignored for long /

(He brushes.)

even by <u>killers</u> <u>who</u> <u>are</u> <u>not</u> /

(They both laugh, and shake.)

I love you so /

(She is resigned but afraid.)

I love you so /

(FEVER lets fall the hairbrush, which clatters. All the time he has been standing behind her, and now throttles her from his position. Her parasol falls, with a second sound. He holds the weight of her head in his hands, and breathes, and recovers, but the head of THOMA remains lovingly in his hands.)

I passed Satan on the road /

(He waits, as if recollecting a fact.)

'you are killing your lover' / he said / 'because you have to know what it is like to have done so' /

(He frowns. His gaze falls to THOMA.)

'no' / I said /

*

IRRESPECTIVE

Characters

ISM   The Tenant of a Lonely Place

NOUS   Another

An old man edges on. He cleans his spectacles. He regards the public with suspicion and contempt.

ISM: I'm not him /

   (He peers out.)

   he's not here /

   (He polishes. He looks out.)

   I'm here / but I'm not him /

   (He might withdraw, but does not.)

   and if I was /

   (He spites the public.)

   I wouldn't /

   (He remains.)

   so there you are /

   (This might seem conclusive, but ISM remains, his gaze on the floor.)

   who do you think you are /

   (His rebuke is mild, tempered by time.)

   who do you /

   (His head shakes pitifully.)

   who /

   (He is resigned, waits, then goes to leave. He stops after a few paces. He seems to want to resume, but denies himself, and is silent. At last he must utter.)

   so you're in trouble /

   (He is unsurprised.)

   you're in trouble / you think /

   (He is oddly amused.)

'we'll go to him' /

(He lifts his gaze to the public.)

unfortunately he isn't here /

(He is cruel in his scrutiny.)

I'm here / but I'm not him /

(He speaks with an icy articulation.)

<u>frustrating</u> /

(He searches their faces.)

<u>frustrating</u> / when you want him / he is not here /

(His smile is unhealthy. He goes to leave again and stops dead, his back to them.)

go to the usual / why don't you /

(He struggles to contain his bitterness.)

plead with them /

(His shoulders tremble with a sub-laugh.)

or /

(The laugh is now unsubdued.)

have the usual fled /

(He sniffs.)

yes / it's a shame he isn't here /

(He gazes skywards.)

I'm here / but I'm not him /

(He waits. Suddenly he exclaims.)

and how typical that is / oh / how typical / how very / how very and so /

(He laughs, and is briefly consumed by the laugh.)

you find yourself in trouble / vicious / deep / and ugly
trouble / and going to the usual / you find the usual
useless /

(He crows.)

<u>useless</u> <u>is</u> <u>the</u> <u>usual</u> /

(He shakes his head in pleasure.)

all right / you say / we'll go to him /

(He is withering.)

<u>not</u> <u>your</u> <u>first</u> <u>choice</u> /

(He waits, staring.)

and he isn't in /

(His smile is cold.)

I'm in / but I'm not him /

(And colder still.)

how very and so /

(His stare intensifies.)

how very and so /

(He baits them.)

<u>typical</u> /

(He luxuriates, then turns to leave again, and again stops.)

when will he be /

(He does not turn.)

when will he /

(He declines to move or speak for a little time, then turns again.)

and you heard he never /

(He bawls.)

how do I know / I'm not him /

(He looks cruelly.)

never sets foot / never / never / so you heard / as if /

(He is unexpectedly forlorn.)

he anticipated the day might come when / the usual having /

(He sniggers.)

as the usual does / betrayed you with its /

(He laughs.)

usualness /

(He stops, sniffs.)

you'd come to him /

(He seems to ponder this proposition. He is not cruel now.)

who do you think you are /

(He shakes his head.)

who do you /

(And looks at the public blankly.)

who /

(He looks down, modestly.)

he's down the shops /

(He stays in this posture for a long time.)

which is to say /

(He lifts his eyes.)

nothing much /

(He plays with time.)

the last time he went down the shops / he was away two years /

(He stares.)

that was a woman /

(And plays.)

now it's eyes / bad eyes / he stumbles / he collides / what with the sinking pavements / and the rising kerbs / you can't assume / when he states / in that matter-of-fact way he has / he's <u>going down the shops</u> / you will ever meet again /

(He smiles thinly.)

frustrating / when you need him / he is /

(He can barely conceal his triumph.)

<u>down the shops</u> /

(This might be an opportune moment to take his leave, but ISM cannot, and he sticks to the ground. His voice is altered by the depths of his resentment.)

and he was here /

(He chews.)

he was here / and you knew that he was here /

(He strains the word.)

<u>always</u> /

(And waits, and strains it further.)

<u>always</u> /

(His face aches.)

always / here /

(He fumes.)

the days stood one upon the other / and the months / a hill
of months / a hill of years / and did you ever / ever / did
you / ever / even once /

(He explodes.)

and you knew that he was here /

(He recovers swiftly. He sniffs. He shrugs.)

the place /

(He shrugs again.)

adequate /

(He chews.)

the tap runs /

(And sniffs.)

adequate /

(He laughs to himself, and ceases. He adopts a tone of resignation.)

no / it's a pity he's not here /

*(His head turns on his neck, once or twice. He cannot resist a further
refinement.)*

or is it /

(He lets time pass. He looks at the ground.)

and he wasn't sorry / no / not at all sorry / that you didn't
come /

(And nods slightly.)

on this / if nothing else / let us be clear / he neither
anticipated / nor craved / your appearance /

(He suddenly shouts.)

you are / I do / do hope / clear /

(And is benign at once.)

he hates misapprehension / hates it whilst /

(He smiles thinly.)

being a man of such / such / being such a man / he could
not fail to recognize the surging tide of ambiguity that flows
against all resolutions of / and statements of / irrefutable /

(He looks.)

etceteras /

(He laughs in a forlorn way.)

no / he did not want you here / and looking at you / if I
were him /

(He is at his cruellest.)

no more would I /

(He is half-polite.)

did it never /

(He hesitates.)

oh /

(But proceeds.)

did it never strike you as the most / quite the most /
extravagant and grotesque / impertinence / to drag your
oozing and suppurating skin of trouble here when /

(He shakes his head in disbelief.)

for years you /

(He shakes it again.)

it demeans me to accuse you /

(The shaking diminishes.)

and that is / surely that is /

(He huffs.)

the very limit of /

(He huffs again.)

<u>contempt</u> /

(He is suddenly cheerful.)

of course he has the answer /

(He is ascendant.)

you know as well as I / he has the answer / the years you consumed / reiterating / disseminating / and / yes / one might say /

(The word is hideous in his mouth.)

<u>believing</u> /

(He licks his mouth to clear it.)

<u>the</u> <u>usual</u> / he used in order to refine /

(He is deeply sarcastic.)

thank you for not interrupting him / so kind / so kind /

(And looks at the public cruelly.)

<u>the</u> <u>answer</u> /

(ISM ponders staying or leaving. He begins to withdraw, but not far.)

obviously / it does not follow / that having discovered <u>the</u> <u>answer</u> / he will have the slightest inclination to impart it / why should he / when you /

(He despises the public.)

clustering at the door / and insolent /

(He twists the knife.)

insolent / and clustering at the door /

(He watches.)

for thirty years ignored him /

(He is supremely contemptuous.)

I wouldn't /

(He measures time.)

but I'm not him /

(He observes the effect of his words on the public. He turns to withdraw. The sound of a slammed door stops him. He is quite still. The door is slammed again, not with irritation, but from familiarity with its bad catch. ISM waits for the third slam. He is unsurprised by the appearance of an old man carrying a linen shopping bag, containing a few items.)

they're in trouble /

(NOUS puts down the bag, and in a routine way, goes out again. He returns with a chair. He sits in the chair. He waits a short time before leaning to the bag and removing an item of grocery. He studies it, as if he were not certain it was the thing he intended to buy. He does not spend time on this, but returns it to the bag. He is still.)

and the usual /

(He waits.)

fancy /

(And again waits.)

the usual / useless /

(He waits.)

fancy /

(He erupts in a short, crapulous laugh. NOUS, his hands on his knees, tilts back his head, and tilts it forward again. He remains

like this for a considerable time. At last he rises to his feet and goes out, without haste.)

he doesn't like you /

(ISM looks complacently at the public.)

any more than I do /

(He is patronizing now.)

and who could / who with any / even the slightest / capacity for discrimination /

(He smiles again.)

like you /

(He watches, witheringly.)

nobody /

(His gaze is not altered by the reappearance of NOUS, who sits as before.)

I said /

(He reflects on the words he will use.)

I said /

(And longer.)

they sense this probably / they are not liked / I was careful not to say we disliked them / I was very careful /

(He waits.)

not to say 'we' /

(And gazes cruelly.)

they are presumptuous / they are insolent / but me /

(He sniffs.)

I'm not /

(ISM is quite still, and so is NOUS. NOUS again leans to the bag and retrieves the same package of grocery. Again he studies the label. Nothing in his manner suggests irritation. At last he returns it to the bag.)

what concerns me /

(NOUS adopts his old posture, gazing up, then down.)

is this /

(He is in no hurry to articulate his concern.)

having come / having dispensed with the services of /

(His mouth struggles.)

the <u>usual</u> /

(He resumes coolly.)

and <u>come</u> /

(He cannot resist.)

thirty years too late I need not say / need I / need I /

(He twists in his rage.)

<u>need</u> I <u>say</u> /

(And ceases.)

why would they ever go away again /

(He gazes into the public, all hostility abolished briefly.)

after all / they have / with that peculiar insight which arrives simultaneously with panic / identified the place / the only place / the answer could possibly be /

(He smiles.)

if you felt like it / if you were so inclined /

(The smile is rigid.)

<u>imparted</u> /

(NOUS says nothing and seems to think nothing.)

this is what concerns me /

(He waits.)

frankly /

(And waits.)

and we like a quiet life /

(He waits. He sways very slightly on his heels.)

or /

(He creates an ironic sound.)

a quiet life is what we have become accustomed to /

(He waits.)

our solitude / until today /

(He plays with sound.)

un / in /

(NOUS dives into the shopping bag again, retrieves the packet and frowning, stares at the label for the third time.)

un / in /

(NOUS, in his exasperation, thrusts the packet at ISM. ISM studies the label. He confirms whatever has discomforted NOUS.)

mmm /

(He nods, as if he shared the surprise of NOUS.)

I'll take it back /

(He completes his sentence.)

un / in / frin /

(He plays.)

ged / ged /

(NOUS stands and taking up the shopping bag, goes out. ISM, holding the packet, calls out to him.)

they're sitting down /

(He is profoundly resentful.)

they're tired of standing up / and they're sitting down /

(His mouth twists.)

not all of them /

(He gazes.)

most / most of them have started sitting down /

(He frowns.)

I was afraid of this /

(Instantly he revises.)

well / not exactly / to say 'I was afraid of this' implies I had / over the years / nourished a dread this moment would arrive / not at all / how could I / or you even / have guessed the <u>usual</u> would / inexorably / have been exposed as <u>useless</u> / the deception might have lingered on for years /

(He is alarmed.)

now they're all /

(He turns to call to NOUS.)

the whole lot / sitting down /

(His apprehension marks his features.)

<u>we're</u> <u>under</u> <u>siege</u> /

(He affects to laugh at his own panic, but the laugh dies in his mouth. He twitches.)

they know you're here /

(He plays with the packet, turning it in his fingers.)

so long as I / and only I / was here / and it was understood
by them / I was not you /

(He is vehement and defensive at once.)

a thing I made abundantly clear / iterating / and
reiterating / I was not you /

(He breathes curiously.)

the situation was /

(He shrugs.)

was / vastly better than it is now /

(He turns the packet round and round.)

the mistake I made / was to admit / casually /

(He writhes.)

stupidly and casually /

(His head twists.)

you were down the shops / so the moment you /

(He is consumed by shame.)

hove into view /

(His shrug is pitiful.)

we aren't / either of us / are we / used to /

(He shakes his head dolefully.)

the phenomenon of others /

(He laughs pitifully.)

whilst having the answer / never expecting to be asked /

(He aches.)

to give the answer /

(NOUS comes back, unhurried as all his movements are. He takes in the spectacle of the public without satisfaction or dread. ISM also gazes. Time passes.)

they won't leave empty-handed / will they /

(NOUS is silent.)

having come this far / and having ascertained that you are here /

(Time passes. ISM chews his tongue in his anxiety.)

the way they / sitting and silent / how long will that last /

(And passes.)

that patient and respectful /

(He shudders.)

that won't last /

(He mocks them.)

'give us the answer' /

(NOUS sniffs.)

bricks through the windows /

(He repeats.)

'give us the answer' /

(And develops his dread.)

cut the water off /

(He tightens his lips. NOUS, without signs of irritation, resumes his seat. ISM stares on until the spectacle is intolerable. He turns to NOUS. His mouth opens and closes, several times. Having failed to

utter, he goes out, and returns at once with a chair which he sets near to NOUS, and with a certain resolution, occupies it.)

I think say something /

(They are still.)

by which I mean nothing at all /

(NOUS heeds but coolly. ISM folds his hands neatly. Time passes.)

you have the answer / but do they deserve it /

(NOUS is silent.)

and would they know the answer from what passes for the answer / after all / for thirty years they did not want the answer /

(And remains so.)

they knew / of course / the answer existed and could be discovered / here / but they preferred the usual / the <u>useless</u> <u>usual</u> / and you / therefore / are relieved of any obligation to supply what they / at this late stage / have decided they are entitled to hear /

(He is uncommonly calm.)

say any trash /

(He is patient.)

the answer cannot be violated simply because this mob / in their extremity / choose to appear /

(And waits.)

what would they do with it anyway /

(And waits.)

I ask you /

(He throws back his head.)

ha /

(He shakes his head.)

the mess /

(And laughs sweetly.)

they would make of the answer /

(He is patronizing.)

frankly / to give <u>the</u> <u>answer</u> / or to parody the answer /
and give them <u>that</u> /

(He is amused.)

would it make any difference /

(His smile fades.)

there's more of them /

(He rises to his feet. He frowns.)

a lot more / and they're shoving / they haven't got the
patience of the first lot /

(He bites his lip in his anxiety.)

there's an altercation going on / they all want the answer /
but whereas the first lot seemed prepared to sit and wait /
this lot /

(His face is screwed tight.)

oh /

(He looks away.)

oh /

(He half-turns back.)

that's / surely that's not /

(He exclaims.)

I'm easily shocked / the quiet life / you forget / don't you /
what so-called human beings are /

(He looks at NOUS, who remains in his stillness.)

capable of /

(He looks at his fist.)

I've crushed the biscuits /

(He is shocked.)

I've crushed the /

(NOUS, rising to his feet, causes the legs of his chair to scrape eerily on the boards. ISM is all nerves.)

she's nice / the woman in the shop / very nice / but will she take them back / I don't think so / and anyway /

(He looks pathetically at NOUS.)

fat chance of /

(He shrugs under the regard of NOUS.)

getting down the shops with all this /

(And falters. He sits.)

going on /

(ISM senses decision in NOUS.)

fat chance /

(NOUS turns dimly towards the world. Time passes, as he collects himself. ISM looks. His offer is worthless, deliberately so.)

I could /

(He falters.)

whatever you are thinking / of doing / or saying / I could / only /

(He looks at the floor.)

I'm not you / and they are perfectly aware that I'm not you /

(He sniffs.)

it was the first thing I said / when they were /

(He is defeated.)

when there were comparatively few of them /

(NOUS is no longer hearing ISM. At last he makes his first shuffle towards the public.)

I think /

(NOUS stops.)

now I think / despite all I just said /

(He looks up.)

give them the answer /

(NOUS is filled with a sense of destiny, a destiny he does not relish. He advances another pace or two.)

if you don't / if you just /

(He frowns.)

extemporize / they /

(An irritated flick of one hand warns ISM to be silent.)

they'll know /

(NOUS, alone as never before, draws breath, and creates a smile of such ambivalence it is surely evidence of his genius. He goes out. The door is closed, fails to catch, and is closed again. Finally, it is slammed. ISM, perched on his chair, waits and watches, the biscuit packet still in his hand. From the distance, a peculiar sound, as the public greets NOUS. It is scarcely applause, nor is it in the least ecstatic. ISM'S pose describes his strain and his curiosity.)

they don't like it /

(Time passes.)

he is giving them the answer / and they don't like it /

(He is bemused in a ghastly way.)

what did he expect / obviously / by definition / the answer
is /

(He squirms.)

<u>repugnant</u> /

(He connects.)

all you can say about the answer / and he knows this / he
knows it better than anyone / is that the answer / when it
is / at last / by threats or blandishments / <u>revealed</u> /

(He is oddly satisfied.)

will not be / cannot be / and possibly / god knows / god
knows / should never be /

(He gasps.)

<u>recognizable</u> /

(And gasps again.)

they hear him / they hear his / all his / beautiful and deep
his /

(He shakes his head.)

and they think he is mocking them / they think he is
indulging in a provocation /

(He is moved by his perception.)

so rotted are they / so corrupted by their addiction to the
usual / they think /

(He is profoundly wounded.)

the answer is /

(The thought tortures him.)

the <u>usual</u> /

(He sneers.)

upside down / back to front / but still /

(He spews the word.)

the usual /

(He jeers.)

they come / by train / by car / they stagger down the
lane / they shove / it rains on them / for what / for what /

(He detects disturbing signs.)

they resent him / they respect him / and resent him / and
the resentment / it's obvious from here / is getting the
upper hand /

(He frets.)

from here / but not from there / perhaps /

(He twitches.)

he's going on / he's /

(He is surprised.)

uncommonly animated / ha /

(He derides himself.)

who wouldn't be / his shoulders and / waving his hands /
he /

(He dislikes the spectacle.)

of course the answer comes in many forms / presumably /
the long / the short / the adumbrated and the /

(Now he observes more coolly.)

he's /

(He is bewildered.)

notwithstanding their resentment / he's /

(He stares.)

you might almost think /

(A strange smile covers his confusion.)

if you didn't know him / if you didn't know his profound contempt for /

(He is certain, briefly.)

influence / communication / persuasion / and all the /

(He falters.)

if you were not familiar with the /

(The certainty decays.)

<u>supreme</u> <u>detachment</u> / which for forty years has characterized this / this /

(He is empty. Time passes.)

but he is /

(His neck stretches.)

he is /

(His face aches.)

<u>enjoying</u> <u>himself</u> /

(ISM is drained. His speech is leaden.)

I can't look / I'm looking / but I can't look /

(Eventually he obeys his own injunction. He staggers back to his chair. He wants to lean on it with both hands but finds himself impeded by the crushed biscuits. He flings the packet to the floor. He leans, utterly weary, on the back of the chair. Time falls away.)

so /

(His gaze is fixed on the ceiling.)

none of us is immune /

(A final wave of rage surges through him, and he shouts.)

they <u>don't</u> <u>even</u> <u>like</u> <u>you</u> /

(His head twists violently.)

they <u>think</u> <u>you</u> <u>are</u> <u>ridiculous</u> /

(He jeers.)

<u>with</u> <u>your</u> <u>arms</u> <u>in</u> <u>the</u> <u>air</u> /

(And hates.)

<u>a</u> <u>parody</u> / <u>a</u> <u>parody</u> <u>of</u> /

(The word is diseased.)

<u>eloquence</u> /

(The hate sinks away.)

what do you care / you have an audience /

(And is replaced by contempt.)

and if they hanged you / you'd say /

(He sings it.)

'<u>I</u> <u>was</u> <u>heard</u>' /

(He laughs weakly.)

as the chair was pulled from under you /

(He scowls.)

'<u>I</u> <u>was</u> <u>heard</u>' /

(His cruelty is cut short by the sound of the door, which is closed twice and then slammed, as before. ISM is stiff with indignation and does not look up as NOUS enters and without reference to ISM, goes down to the place from which ISM had observed the scene. He puts his hands in his coat pockets. He gazes, perfectly still.)

with respect /

(ISM is resolute.)

with what's left of my respect / I have to say / I never thought I'd see the day /

(NOUS turns to regard ISM, who can't bear his scrutiny.)

'he's not here' / I said /

(He shrugs.)

ha /

(He is morose.)

'he's not here' /

(He stares at the floor.)

I should have said 'for thirty years he was / but now he's not /

(He is at his bitterest.)

someone is / but it's not him' /

(He looks up into NOUS.)

but how was I to know you were no longer him /

(NOUS is blank, uncritical. Their antagonism is sustained.)

yes /

(ISM intuits NOUS'S rebuke and counter attacks.)

I did / I did encourage you / but I was scared / I thought / they'll break the windows / they'll cut the water off /

(He watches NOUS.)

but I'm weak /

(He is strangely arrogant.)

weak but you / you're not /

(He is unashamed.)

you might so easily have defied my weakness / saying /

(He imagines.)

saying / <u>your</u> nerves <u>belong</u> <u>to</u> <u>you</u> /

(He admires the thought.)

<u>supreme</u> <u>disdain</u> /

(He nods again and again.)

I would have got the point /

(NOUS, without responding by word or look, goes to his chair and sits, his hands still in his pockets, his gaze still on ISM.)

but you went / you went down / you went down carrying the answer / the long / the short / the adumbrated version / I don't know which /

(ISM is deeply wounded.)

and /

(He affects incredulity.)

and /

(He finds the worst word yet.)

<u>satisfied</u> them /

(He nods.)

the thirty years I thought was a wall / a wall of pain / of subtlety / and neglect /

(He pulls a face.)

was not a wall /

(NOUS heeds all ISM says, without responding to it.)

it was a sheet /

(ISM fears nothing now.)

and you / you / up on your hind legs like a circus dog /

(He could sob.)

tore the sheet to ribbons /

(NOUS absorbs ISM'S verdict without evident discomfort. His eyes fall on the packet of smashed biscuits. ISM'S pain is not yet spent out. He must continue.)

<u>irrespective</u> / you would say /

(He moistens his lips. He does not look at NOUS.)

<u>irrespective</u> / your spasm of vanity / your susceptibility to / what shall we call it /

(He loathes.)

<u>acclaim</u> /

(He shudders.)

that wasn't acclaim /

(He returns to the subject.)

it's not however / is it / <u>irrespective</u> /

(And loads the words.)

<u>to</u> <u>the</u> <u>answer</u> /

(He twists the knife.)

because / if it was the answer / and you possessed it / you could not have given it in the way you did /

(ISM is in an agony of indignation.)

a man who / at the crisis of his life / reveals himself to be rotten through and through with vanity / could never / ever / have discovered the answer in the first place /

(He is supreme.)

thirty years so what / he is disqualified /

(And melancholy.)

if it was the answer / they should have had to drag it out of you with red-hot pincers /

(NOUS in his usual unhurried way, gets up and goes to the packet, bends, and picks it up.)

she won't take them back / not in that state /

(NOUS drifts out. ISM is silent at last. Odd sounds of domesticity. NOUS returns with the identical shopping bag, the packet inside. ISM cannot meet his eyes. NOUS is still, gazing down. It is as if he might offer a defence to all that has been said and is framing it. But he does not utter, and goes out. The awkward door is closed three times. Time passes. At last ISM stands and goes down to observe.)

they cleared off / anyway /

(He stares forlornly.)

that's something /

(He fights a great sob that rises through him, and overcomes it. He blinks a tear.)

probably /

*

DISTANCE

'We passed through ruined villages and devastated farms, and when I asked, where are the people, I was told there were none, the men having been killed in the war, and the women driven far and wide. And when I enquired as to the cause of this terrible war, the guide said no one could remember, but once it had begun, neither side could end it, because the sacrifice of so many not only justified but demanded the expenditure of yet more lives. And so it went on. I wept to think of this perpetual war, the uselessness of which has become legendary.'

'I do not doubt the spectacle you describe was heartbreaking, but strictly speaking, if it became the source of a legend, how could it be properly described as useless?'

Chian H'si '<u>Conversations with Hu</u>'
(circa 1380)

Characters

STONE   The Mother

FETCH   The Friend

BRODY   The Son

1

A room in 1918. A woman enters. She moves briskly, as if summoned there, and stops, as if alerted by a distant sound, perhaps imaginary. Her intense concentration. Her infinite stillness, broken at last by her cry.

STONE: He's dead then / he's dead / he's dead /

(Nothing transpires. She flings a few paces and is still again.)

Dead /

(She weighs the word, the thought.)

Dead / I said /

(She calls.)

DEAD /

(She plucks her fingers, and calls again.)

HE'S DEAD /

(The silence is intense. She sways in it, a sapling in a gale, then stills herself.)

By the way /

(And calls.)

BY THE WAY / HE'S /

(She stops and starts.)

DEAD / HE'S /

(She plays.)

DEAD / HE'S / DEAD / HE'S /

(She is amused and appalled.)

DEAD / BY THE WAY / HE'S / BY THE WAY / HE'S /

(She sways, laughing.)

By the way / by the way / by the way he's /

(She calls.)

BY THE WAY /

(And tortures the words.)

DEAD / HE'S / DEAD / HE'S / BY THE WAY HE'S / DEAD / DEAD / AND / BY THE WAY / HE'S /

(She smiles. She shakes her head.)

By the way he's /

(She recovers. She arranges her fingers in her hands. A second woman, aghast, strides into the room. She stares at STONE, her mouth puckered. She is unable to speak. STONE continues to examine her fingers. She abandons this and crosses the floor, her movements agile, easy, and stops.)

It's all right /

(They are both still, looking in opposite directions.)

Perfectly /

(She tilts back her head very slightly.)

PERFECTLY ALL RIGHT /

(FETCH turns her head violently towards STONE, as if to rebuke this.)

IT IS / IT IS / IT IS ALL RIGHT /

(Her authority suffocates any protest FETCH might have made. They glare, a contest ended by STONE'S order.)

Chair /

(FETCH does not move at once.)

CHAIR FOR ME /

(Now she does, and marches out and back with an upright chair. She places it, and STONE sits. FETCH remains with her hands on the chair back. STONE proceeds to articulate a thesis.)

Slung between my hips a womb / you too / between
yours / slung / a womb /

(She meditates briefly.)

And all / all women /

(She invents a term and enjoys it.)

WOMBSLUNG / ALL OF US /

(She moistens her lips, thoughtfully.)

One night of love / or not-love / say a night of not-love /
mostly not / mostly not-love / you / me / everyone /

(She lifts a hand, and it falls.)

This /

*(She lets out a descriptive cry, as of a sexual climax, and shudders.
This also faintly amuses her.)*

And /

*(She rises to her feet, and in an imitation of the annunciation,
indicates her belly with both hands. Now she laughs. The laugh
slowly fades. FETCH is anxious for her.)*

These /

(She frowns.)

BANAL MIRACLES /

(In the following silence, FETCH lifts a kind hand to STONE'S face.)

No /

*(Biting her lip, FETCH withdraws the hand. STONE collapses the
image of the annunciation, and sits again.)*

2

Time passes.

STONE: It's a /

> *(She moistens her lips again in the same way.)*

We need not /

> *(She fights herself.)*

It's a / a /

> *(She places the tips of her fingers together, as if it might strengthen her.)*

It's a /

> *(She looks down for the word.)*

Servitude /

> *(And lifts her head.)*

Don't you think / a servitude / to which we need not /

> *(She launches herself off the chair and flings, and stops.)*

I / I / not you / me /

> *(She makes fists of her hands.)*

I need not give assent /

> *(FETCH studies STONE.)*

YOU CAN / WHO'S STOPPING YOU / ASSENT / ASSENT /

FETCH: *(Exasperated.)* ASSENT TO WHAT /

> *(FETCH'S tone compels STONE to utter her thesis starkly.)*

STONE: These clay things / these churning clays /

> *(She lists them.)*

Desire / the act / the birth / maternity /

(Now she makes a tight mouth.)

GRIEF /

(FETCH is stronger than STONE for a moment.)

FETCH: Your son is dead / you must grieve /

(STONE'S regard is unfaltering. At last she speaks.)

STONE: <u>You</u> grieve /

(FETCH wavers as if struck a blow.)

FETCH: I will /

STONE: Good /

FETCH: I WILL GRIEVE /

STONE: Good /

(The women stare. FETCH shakes her head in her despair.)

Good I said /

(FETCH suffers for them both.)

FETCH: HOLD ME /

(STONE shakes her head in contempt.)

oh / hold me and be held /

(STONE declines this invitation with a measured look. FETCH recovers her equilibrium.)

The telegram / might I /

(She half-shrugs.)

I'd like to see the telegram /

(She bites her lip, as if having confessed something shameful, trivial.)

The words / the form of the words I'd /

STONE: It's still to come /

FETCH: The telegram is still to /

STONE: THE TELEGRAM IS YET TO COME / WHEN IT COMES
YOU MAY READ IT / YOU MAY STUDY THE FORM OF
THE WORDS / YOU MAY PUT IT UNDER GLASS OR / IF
YOU PREFER / BENEATH YOUR PILLOW / WHERE / WITH
THE PASSAGE OF THE YEARS / IT WILL DISINTEGRATE
/ TELEGRAMS BEING FLIMSY / FLIMSY PRESUMABLY
BECAUSE NOTHING THEY ANNOUNCE IS WORTHY OF
PRESERVATION / THE INSIGNIFICANCE OF THE FACTS
THAT THEY COMMUNICATE / 'YOUR SON IS DEAD' /
TO TAKE JUST ONE / MUNDANE EXAMPLE / SCARCELY
ENTITLES THEM TO BE INSCRIBED ON EXQUISITE HAND-
MADE PAPER /

FETCH: That is not the reason /

STONE: ISN'T IT /

FETCH: The reason telegrams are /

STONE: WHAT IS THE REASON / THEN? /

(FETCH feels foolish and shakes her head swiftly.)

FETCH: This is silly /

STONE: *(Stamping her foot.)* WHAT IS THE REASON? /

(FETCH is unwilling to comply with STONE'S demand, but concedes.)

FETCH: The telegraph boy has a /

(She stops.)

This is so silly /

(She resumes under STONE'S intense scrutiny.)

Has a small pouch slung across his shoulder /

STONE: Yes /

FETCH: And rides a bicycle /

STONE: Yes /

(STONE is adamant, driving FETCH further.)

FETCH: If the telegrams were printed on a superior quality of paper /

(She is humiliated.)

STONE: Also the envelopes /

FETCH: Also the envelopes / as befits the gravity of the communication /

STONE: Yes /

FETCH: Then /

(She feels unable to proceed.)

STONE: *(Without sarcasm.)* The pouch would need to be that much bigger /

FETCH: Yes /

STONE: Would need / in fact / not to be a pouch at all / but something like a / a /

FETCH: Satchel /

STONE: A satchel / yes /

(STONE seems satisfied.)

That's logical / perfectly logical /

(She seems lifted by this clarification.)

What's more / given the sheer volume of telegrams generated by the war / like leaves shed in a windy Autumn / I doubt / I really doubt / even a satchel would be adequate /

(They exchange a long, mild look.)

Imagine the weight / the poor boy's shoulders as he cycled /

(She shakes her head, a smile on her lips.)

No / they <u>must</u> be flimsy /

(A long look is sustained between them.)

FETCH: So /

(FETCH bites her lip.)

In actual fact /

(STONE breaks the composition by walking a little.)

As yet there is no telegram /

(STONE'S reply is to take a few more steps. Then she turns to examine FETCH. FETCH is rational.)

You have had an intuition / an appalling intuition / this intuition / obviously / cannot be confirmed /

(She is determined to be kind.)

Nor /

(She tightens her mouth, as if she might say too much.)

Nor needs to be /

(She looks to STONE for confirmation.)

Is that the case? /

(STONE'S silence invites FETCH to complete the speculation herself, which she does by nodding.)

This deep / so deep / oh / very / very deep /

(STONE abolishes FETCH'S meditation on maternity before it has begun by briskly leaving.)

STONE: Clear out his room / will you /

(FETCH goes to protest, but STONE calls back to her.)

I CAN'T / I CAN'T /

3

FETCH is alone and still for a long time. Then she shouts.

FETCH: SHE CAN'T / SHE CAN'T /

(Time passes. It is as if FETCH predicted the return of STONE.)

SHE CAN'T /

(The non-appearance of STONE incites FETCH, who hurries to the door and shouts.)

SHE CAN'T /

(Her boldness causes her to laugh, shrilly. She returns, with slower steps. She gazes ahead. Her fingers lift to the buttons of her shirt. She proceeds to unfasten one after another. Having completed this, she draws the shirt off her shoulders. She waits. She then lifts the straps of her bra away from her shoulders. Her breasts are exposed. Her hands fall to her sides.)

I said /

(She interrupts herself.)

Funny phrase / what's it like out there / out there / funny phrase / <u>out</u> there /

(She ponders this.)

If he were / say / on holiday / in Rome / in Spain / in Sicily / would you say / you wouldn't / would you? / say / <u>out</u> there / you'd say / there / <u>there</u> / you'd say / what's it like <u>there</u> / not / <u>out</u> there / out there is different / out there means / horrid / it's horrid out there / this is /

(She chews thoughtfully.)

This is our kindness / a kindness / we perform without knowing it /

(She is still, then violent.)

THAT'S THE ONLY KINDNESS / THE ONLY / ONLY
KINDNESS /

(The vehemence shakes her. She restores herself, then suddenly, as if shocked.)

MY HAIR IS UP / MY HAIR IS /

(Immediately she drags the pins from her hair, which cascades. She tosses it. Then still again, luxuriates in this image of mourning.)

I can't say / he said / I can't explain to you / who's not been there / what it is like / out there / try / I said / he shook his head / please try / he would not try /

(She recollects the hour.)

This not-trying / this not-even-trying / wounded me /

(The word seems ill-chosen.)

WOUNDED /

(She creates a weak laugh, and at once abolishes it.)

As if I lacked imagination / or /

(She proclaims.)

WHAT'S WORSE /

(She suffers this.)

Could not be trusted with the gift of his experience / as if / as if / in even attempting to communicate this / this /

(She waves a futile hand.)

OUT THERE /

(The hand is fixed in the air.)

The profundity of his pain would be demeaned /

(Her hand falls slowly.)

I call that unkind / I do / unkind /

(FETCH is aware that STONE has appeared in the doorway and is studying her. Both women guard their decisions. At last STONE speaks.)

STONE: I'll clear the room /

(FETCH is still.)

My son's room / I'll clear the room myself /

(FETCH lowers her head fractionally.)

In saying I could not clear his room I was / and even as I said it I sensed this / contradicting myself / and by implication / admitting nothing I had said up till then was heartfelt / but all of it was /

FETCH: Yes /

STONE: Some argument contrived by me to smother /

FETCH: Yes /

STONE: An agony I would not admit to /

FETCH: That is how it seemed to me /

STONE: Whereas /

FETCH: *(An irresistible exclamation.)* Whereas /

(FETCH'S contempt causes STONE to flinch.)

whereas /

(She shakes her head, a condescension. STONE walks further into the room. She observes FETCH'S condition.)

STONE: You have exposed your breasts /

(FETCH is unabashed.)

With or without a telegram /

FETCH: *(Acute to sarcasm.)* A mother's intuition / with regard to her son's death / is conclusive / and if she will not mourn / should that /

(She is swept by a wave of nausea.)

WHY SHOULD THAT INHIBIT ME /

(She stares rigidly at the floor, her hair hanging over her face, a classical image of grief. STONE is not unkind in her regard. This alone evinces a torrent of sobs from FETCH. She shudders. The spectacle creates no impulse in STONE, who frowns but makes no move.)

Touch me / oh / touch me /

(STONE declines to do so.)

Oh / touch me /

(STONE concedes nothing. FETCH recovers her breath, and her composure. Her fingers return to her buttons. She covers herself, without haste.)

STONE: I /

(She ponders, and paces.)

My /

(FETCH tosses her hair, and fixes it behind her head.)

My /

(STONE is unable to articulate. She gazes at the floor. FETCH completes her dress. She attends.)

I /

(Again she stops. Now she lifts a frank, open gaze to FETCH.)

I have no desire / please say you understand this / I should like you to understand it / no desire to shield myself from the appalling pain a mother would expect to suffer as a consequence of her son's death / I am not /

(She shudders faintly, a frisson of confession.)

I do want you to believe me /

(She shakes her head briefly.)

I am not resorting to outlandish stratagems / intellectual or psychological / to preserve my equilibrium from a deluge of emotion I sense I cannot cope with /

(STONE challenges FETCH with her regard.)

HOWL / YOU SAY / HOWL /

(She tightens her fists.)

I do not wish to howl /

(She looks yet deeper into FETCH.)

blame / you say / blame if you can't weep /

(Her mouth is a tightened string.)

I blame nobody /

(Now STONE falters.)

There's something else /

(She frowns.)

There is / and it is neither logic nor emotion /

(She is almost pitiful.)

There is / there is /

(FETCH is daunted by the agonized sincerity of STONE'S enquiry, but not understanding it, can only nod her head, a gesture STONE knows the futility of, but does not criticize.)

If he /

(She falters.)

If he / if I were wrong and he /

(She abolishes the possibility.)

He can't / he can't / but if /

(She is resolute.)

Were he to come back through the door /

(FETCH is in dread of the speculation.)

I should not be glad /

(FETCH is deluged by horror, and STONE retracts.)

GLAD / OBVIOUSLY GLAD /

(And persists.)

YET NOT GLAD /

(Having confirmed this, STONE recoils from FETCH'S appalled gaze, and turns her back to her. In this hiatus, STONE recovers some of her objectivity.)

Why? /

(FETCH is unable or unwilling to accompany STONE in her terrible investigation and resorts to a cliché.)

FETCH: Shock / the way shock /

STONE: *(Not unkindly.)* Not shock /

(STONE knows her solitude.)

Thank you but not shock / I've seen shock / the woman with five sons / Mrs / Mrs / holds her hand up / the fingers stretched /

FETCH: Tochter / Mrs Tochter /

STONE: Tochter / yes / five fingers at the window / that's shock / the hand / the eyes / five dead /

(STONE is implacable.)

Necessary / obviously /

FETCH: *(Appalled.)* Necessary? /

STONE: *(Finding the word again.)* Necessary / yes /

FETCH: To win the war? /

STONE: Or lose it / yes /

(FETCH simply gawps at STONE, who rebukes her with her old vehemence.)

 Your indignation / it's /

FETCH: *(Indignant as described.)* TELL HER / TELL THE WOMAN AT THE WINDOW /

STONE: It's /

FETCH: THE WOMAN WITH HER FIVE /

STONE: I know what it is /

FETCH: HER FIVE DEAD /

STONE: It's cowardice /

FETCH: YOUR DEAD SONS ARE PROPERLY DEAD /

STONE: Your indignation is cowardice /

FETCH: SHE'D PLUCK THE EYES OUT OF YOUR HEAD /

(FETCH is exhausted and ashamed.)

I should go / I /

STONE: Yes /

FETCH: I can't / I just can't /

STONE: No /

FETCH: Be here and /

STONE: It's terrible for you /

(FETCH shakes her head.)

In the little castle of your indignation / trembling behind the gate /

FETCH: *(With a pathetic wave of one hand.)* Hearing this / this /

STONE: WHAT NEVER MUST BE HEARD /

(FETCH'S hand drops with a slap to her side.)

One would think it was your son who /

(She stops.)

What is the word / we can expect / it's happening already / this profusion of words /

(She reflects briefly.)

WHO FELL /

(She creates a smile.)

Fell's the word /

(She grimaces.)

In some filthy place / littered with bandages /

FETCH: It's /

STONE: Do go / do go /

FETCH: It's /

STONE: *(A fine, neat gesture.)* Do go /

FETCH: INCOMPREHENSIBLE /

STONE: It's meant to be / now go because / the / I must be honest / the poverty of your imagination somehow / I can't be delicate / contaminates my own / I can't be delicate /

FETCH: *(Wounded.)* I'm poor / I am so /

STONE: Yes /

FETCH: POOR / POOR / I AM POOR / I KNOW /

STONE: Yes / you are /

FETCH: *(Indulging herself.)* SO POOR /

STONE: We have established this / now go /

(FETCH runs from the room. STONE, as if relieved of a suffocating burden, takes extravagant breaths, walking and inhaling. When she is settled, she stops. Suddenly, FETCH lurches in again, a picture of wretched self-loathing.)

No / no /

(FETCH sobs and flees for the second time.)

4

STONE adjusts her fingers, as if this might calm her nerves. Her son walks in, without haste, and sits in the chair. He crosses one leg over the other, and looks at the floor, clasping his hands around his raised knee, as if attending an interview. Time passes, and STONE is unhurried.

STONE: Fell / I said / he fell /

(BRODY makes a bemused sound. Still STONE does not turn to her son.)

FELL /

(This time he makes no response.)

I don't mind fell / a poet thought of it / a poet thought of fell /

(She reflects.)

When / I don't know / in the days of /

(She shrugs.)

So long ago we've lost all /

(And shrugs again.)

The Spartans / they / oh / certainly / they <u>fell</u> /

(Her mouth moves, tightens, hangs, tightens again.)

I want to die / I want to die /

(She aches.)

IF YOU COULD LIVE / TEN DYINGS /

(She is nearly but not quite overwhelmed.)

That is what I am supposed to feel / and /

(She flings up a hand, carelessly.)

You see I feel it / but /

(Her conclusiveness amuses BRODY. At last she faces him.)

There's something else /

(He does not raise his eyes. Her gaze on him is the most refined and tender ever given, a broken maternity but not contained in its maternity. BRODY feels its depth, even its complexity.)

If you were not perfect / to me / and to the world /

(She searches, and searches.)

How could it /

(She yearns.)

It is necessary / your perfection / as your fall is also necessary / both /

(BRODY is contemplative, immaculately so. But STONE is alone, knowing he cannot fathom her. She stares, as if she could make meaning from his beauty and his submission. The effort causes her to lift both hands to her head. She places her fingers on her brow. Now BRODY rises to his feet. His look to her is uncritical.)

You cannot / how could you / and I don't ask / I don't ask you to understand /

(She pleads for his permission.)

But me /

(She frowns across the gulf between them.)

I must / and can /

(BRODY'S look to his mother is tolerant, but in its depths, injured. Slowly he turns and leaves the way he came. STONE reels, as if she would follow him but must not. She finds an equilibrium.)

At the cost of seeming / seeming-or-being /

(She tightens her fists.)

Inhuman /

(The word, then the idea, establishes itself in her.)

I'M NOT HUMAN / IT APPEARS /

(She needs, and finds, the chair.)

ME / ME / I LACK /

(She half-rises off the chair, and falls back.)

I LACK HUMANITY / SO /

(She organizes her thoughts.)

Given this lack / this / this / sickness or perversity / it's perfectly pointless / is it not / to indict me with / to fling in my face / this catalogue of / this inventory of /

(She squirms.)

THE CONSTITUENTS OF COMMON HUMANITY /

(She stands abruptly.)

IT CAN'T APPLY /

(FETCH enters, discreetly. STONE turns to her.)

He's furious /

(FETCH is bewildered, and bites her lip.)

Ashamed and furious /

(STONE places her fingertips together.)

How discreet he was / how careful not to let it show / but /

(She is nostalgic briefly.)

I know my son /

(FETCH is anxious for STONE.)

He was thinking / I could see it in his eyes / my mother / why won't she howl? /

(She is amused.)

THEY DID IN SPARTA / HOW THEY HOWLED THERE /

(She is mild.)

Or /

(She turns as if to silence FETCH.)

Because we're modern / collect the widows / the widows and the black-eyed mothers / and filling the square say /

(She makes her mouth a beak.)

TIME TO END THE ENDLESS WAR /

(FETCH is apprehensive.)

I'm doing neither / am I? /

(FETCH shakes her head.)

Those who are human / they / they / they /

(She did not intend the sentence to be finished. FETCH lets a little time pass. She shrugs uncomfortably. She turns to go.)

You're quitting /

(FETCH stops. She ponders a decision already arrived at.)

FETCH: I think so /

(She aches.)

There's nothing like / nothing quite so / withering / as knowing / and you have this made perfectly clear to me / you are /

(She lifts a hand.)

THOROUGHLY WORTHLESS TO ANOTHER WHOSE PAIN
YOU WOULD SO LIKE TO /

(And lets it fall.)

Oh / what / alleviate by sharing or /

(She yields.)

I don't know /

(FETCH creates an unhealthy smile of renunciation.)

STONE: Perhaps you do /

(She looks at FETCH.)

Alleviate it /

(FETCH is surprised.)

But go if you want to /

(FETCH frowns.)

Go / do go /

FETCH: How / when all you do is /

STONE: *(Irritably.)* THAT'S HOW /

(FETCH is incredulous.)

By ridiculing / despising / and humiliating you / I /

FETCH: *(Provoked.)* WELL / NO / NO TO THAT / THAT /

STONE: *(Smiling.)* SO HOW IS IT YOU WISH TO DO THIS /
THIS / ALLEVIATION / AS YOU CALL IT /

(FETCH is open-mouthed.)

Only in a way that gratifies you / evidently /

(Now STONE rises to her feet.)

I LOSE MY SON / MY ONE SON / AND YOU /

(She sits at once, ashamed.)

No / no / that's so / that's worthless / crude / manipulative / I use my pain to flagellate you / I disgust myself / go / go /

(FETCH does not go.)

Just go /

(STONE gnaws her hand.)

Just go /

(FETCH knows this is scarcely sincere.)

FETCH: It's perfectly true /

STONE: *(Turning in her chair, presenting her back.)* Go now /

FETCH: Perfectly true that I / not only me / perhaps / it might be universal /

(STONE makes an impatient move on the chair.)

In extending my pity to another /

STONE: Another /

FETCH: In extending my pity to you /

(She works out the thought.)

Do so on conditions /

(She shrugs.)

Yes / it's / undeniable /

(She frowns.)

PITY PRESUMES /

(She is resolute.)

I am here for you and you /

STONE: *(In her own thought.)* When I say /

FETCH: You must use me as you wish /

STONE: When I <u>more</u> than say /

FETCH: ENTIRELY AS YOU WISH /

(She seems to brace herself. STONE takes this in, but indifferently.)

STONE: <u>More</u> than say / it isn't <u>saying</u> any more / when I /

(She finds the mot juste.)

<u>Announce</u> /

(She stands for the reiteration of the statement.)

<u>There is something else</u> /

(She addresses FETCH now.)

Other than howling / other than blame /

(She is content with a discovery.)

I am myself afraid of what the something else might be /

(She issues a short uncanny laugh.)

THAT MUST ALWAYS BE THE CASE WITH /

(And is serious again.)

Unwelcome thoughts / surely? /

(She studies FETCH.)

THEIR GRAVITY / THEIR DENSITY / THEIR CAPACITY TO /

(She laughs the same uncanny laugh.)

You see / even now / I am postponing the announcement /

(FETCH nods her head, wanting to keep abreast of STONE. STONE'S eyes fix hers.)

I SQUIRM /

(FETCH bites her lip.)

I DITHER /

(She is afraid of STONE.)

I PREVARICATE /

(Now STONE laughs.)

How human I am / how very human after all / what more human than this delay-upon-delay /

(She sees BRODY enter the doorway and lean on the frame, observing her.)

The dead even / the peculiar reluctance of the dead /

(STONE is herself afraid. Her mouth dry, so she must moisten her lips.)

They / they more than the living /

(FETCH frets for STONE.)

DO NOT WANT TO KNOW /

(She frowns.)

It's / obviously / it's intimidating / they / in their sullen way / they /

FETCH: The dead? /

STONE: INTIMIDATE ME / YES /

FETCH: With what? /

STONE: Oh /

(She trembles.)

Oh /

FETCH: Are they angry? /

STONE: Not angry /

FETCH: Not angry? /

STONE: ANGRY / NO /

(Her eyes are on BRODY.)

DESPAIR / THEIR BOTTOMLESS DESPAIR /

(She drags her eyes from her son to FETCH.)

FETCH: Do not announce it / then /

(STONE is amazed to hear this from FETCH.)

Do not announce what / in any case / you say you have
not / so far /

(She falters.)

As yet /

(STONE is aghast.)

THIS KNOWLEDGE / DON'T /

*(STONE receives this as a wound, and is weakened. She pulls her
fingers, one after another. FETCH is earnest.)*

GIVE US OUR CONSOLATIONS /

*(STONE is at bay, her self-belief bruised by FETCH'S appeal to
common kindness. Her shoulders droop.)*

If you won't console yourself /

*(STONE seems limp. FETCH, ashamed of her proposition, leans on
the back of the empty chair, gazing at the floor. BRODY turns as if
to depart from a scene of painful disharmony, but cannot, and is
suspended in mid-move. The trio are a composition of irresolution.
STONE dreams.)*

5

STONE: I took a train through bandages / so very slow this train / the wheels / the springs / shrill on curves / and on slight gradients it moaned / the filth reached everywhere / to the limits of my eye / no living thing / or wind even / to lift or flick the bandages / the flung / or draped / the piled / or caught-on-thorn / and stiff with filth / coagulated and encrusted / bandages / I asked myself ridiculous questions / such as why bandages are white / why in the first place white / a sensible alternative might be / surely / red / bright / or / because when it is dry blood's brown / brown / I /

(She is silent for some time.)

And out of nowhere came this one / one / out the desolation / hopping / skirting / vaulting obstacles / as if to grab this train as it crept by / and ran beside it / looking up at me / the solitary passenger / as I looked out / he kept up / his cap crushed in one hand / and his mouth open / but saying nothing / breathless possibly but not trying to leap onto the board / and after a while / he fell behind / I watched him standing / and this shout came / this one word shouted /

(STONE seems hurt.)

TELL /

(All three of them are still. STONE moves away, and turns to address both BRODY and FETCH.)

Tell what? /

(She rages and mocks at once.)

TELL THE HORROR OF THE BANDAGES? /

(She is calm at once, by an effort of will.)

That will be known / oh / known and known / and too
well known /

(She looks at FETCH.)

Forgive me my knowledge /

(FETCH is puzzled.)

Do I appall you? / it needs forgiving / obviously /

(FETCH is apprehensive.)

FORGIVE IT OR I DON'T THINK I CAN SPEAK /

(FETCH croaks inaudibly.)

Didn't hear you /

FETCH: I forgive you /

STONE: Do you? / Thank you / thank you for forgiving me /

(STONE imitates humility.)

Peculiar that she who / the one with / who has the will / I
DON'T CALL IT COURAGE / I DON'T FLATTER MYSELF /
the will to know / should stoop to those who / dim / timid
/ and inert / prefer their ignorance /

FETCH: *(Mild in her sarcasm.)* Like me? /

STONE: Like you / yes /

(She knows FETCH'S sarcasm.)

AND THAT'S WHY / WHY I MUST BEG OF YOU YOUR
TOLERANCE OF MY /

(She struggles.)

DISTANCE /

(She sees BRODY go to move.)

DON'T GO /

(He hesitates.)

Oh / don't go / it is so / so / lonely / lonely if you all go /

(She rebukes him.)

YOU ARE LESS LONELY WHERE YOU ARE / LESS LONELY / ALL OF YOU / HORIZONTAL THE FALLEN / I DO KNOW /

(BRODY is patient. STONE inhales profoundly.)

And I could march also / with the mothers / the mothers and the revolutionaries / I could hang the rest of my life from a slogan /

(She is forlorn.)

Something stops me /

FETCH: What I do forgive you for / and would have forgiven / freely / whether or not you had implored me / is your /

STONE: *(Dreading FETCH'S analysis.)* I KNOW / I KNOW /

FETCH: DO YOU / DO YOU KNOW /

STONE: MY / YES / MY /

(She shakes her head violently.)

OF COURSE I KNOW MY /

(She withholds.)

My arrogance / what you call arrogance / my presumption / what you call presumption / my contempt for / what you call contempt /

(She is icy in her counter-attack.)

What other shelter is there / I drag these things across my nakedness as /

(She is briefly self-conscious.)

Yes / I dare say it / as shelled soldiers snatch buckets and tin things to shield their heads /

(She is unabashed.)

I also am exposed /

(And regards FETCH dispassionately.)

Pitiful / of course / the shrapnel just goes in /

(As if conceding something, BRODY, who seemed about to quit the doorway, comes into the room, and stands before his mother, his head tilted slightly to one side, an unposed question. STONE is awed by his proximity, then raises one hand to his tunic button.)

6

She loosens the button, and goes to the next.

STONE: The something else is this /

(She stops. She closes her eyes.)

The something else /

(She opens her eyes, which ache, and extends her hand again to make BRODY naked by degrees.)

Is this /

(She stops, her hand outstretched.)

That /

BRODY: A schoolchild came into the room /

(This intervention halts STONE, but also causes her to smile.)

STONE: She did / and said /

(She laughs very faintly in her shoulder.)

And said /

(She is reluctant to proceed, but feels BRODY'S encouragement.)

'The Pity of War' /

(She hesitates, her hand still to the tunic button.)

To which the teacher said / 'good' /

BRODY: 'Good' / he said /

(She loosens this button. She opens the tunic, to see his naked chest, and gasps from love.)

STONE: And /

(In her bitterness she turns from BRODY.)

They read poems / by soldiers / soldiers who moaned /

(She suffers.)

Moaned pitifully /

BRODY: 'Good' / the teacher said /

(STONE returns to her task, her eyes searching the face of BRODY. At the last button she ceases. She looks down. She laughs, uncannily.)

FETCH: *(Exasperated.)* IT IS GOOD /

(STONE laughs a little more, not in response to FETCH but in pursuance of her own thought.)

GOOD / GOOD / SURELY /

(Ignoring FETCH, STONE lifts her eyes to BRODY. She proceeds to lift his tunic off his shoulders. It falls away. STONE tentatively lifts a hand to his body.)

I call that good /

(And places it on him. She shudders. Her laugh, which is her despair, ripples in her. She lays her cheek to his body.)

A good thing that children understand the horror of and the futility of /

(She shakes in her conviction.)

OBVIOUSLY GOOD /

(STONE, her head on her son's shoulder, chooses words as a bricklayer selects or discards bricks.)

STONE: To die for nothing / is not futile /

(She hears her own words.)

I announce /

(She comes away from BRODY'S body to look at FETCH.)

FUTILITY DOES NOT DETRACT /

(FETCH gawps as STONE articulates.)

THAT IS THE SOMETHING ELSE / THAT /

(Stating this, STONE is replenished.)

How could he / running / tripping / his boots caught up in sordid bandages / how could he know /

(She is inspired.)

HOW COULD HE /

(She implores FETCH.)

TELL / TELL HE BEGGED /

(She raises her open hands.)

TELL WHAT? / THAT YOU SUFFER UNCOMPREHENDINGLY? / THAT YOUR MISERY MAKES NO SENSE? /

(She is calm in her self-possession.)

Oh / that will be told /

BRODY: 'Good' / said the teacher /

STONE: The pity of it / told and told /

BRODY: 'Good' /

STONE: Until the children sicken from the telling /

BRODY: 'Good' / the teacher said /

STONE: HOW COULD HE KNOW THE VERY SENSELESSNESS WOULD /

(She breathes.)

Charm / delight / and ravish /

(She tightens her lips.)

RAVISH / YES /

(And is satisfied.)

The unkilled / the unwasted /

BRODY: 'Good' /

STONE: Listen /

(She appeals to FETCH for understanding.)

If the dead were not so chewed by guns they washed into the ground /

(She is fluent with her vision.)

The living would exhume their bodies / and make a paste out of their flesh /

FETCH: Shh /

STONE: Yes / and spread it on wafers /

FETCH: Oh / shh /

STONE: Oh yes /

(She announces.)

OH / YES /

(She draws her gaze from FETCH back to BRODY.)

BRODY: 'Good' / the teacher says /

STONE: An appetite / insatiable / this appetite /

(She half-smiles.)

THEY'D EAT MY SON /

(Studying him, STONE weeps.)

FETCH: How is it you /

(FETCH withholds her own weeping by immense will.)

It humbles me how you /

(She falters and perseveres.)

Can be both in your grief / and out of it / I watch you wade through your agony / as if it were a stream / a stream of blood / and haul yourself / oh / the weight of your blood-sodden garments / haul yourself onto the other bank /

(She snorts a tear.)

SO LONELY THERE /

(STONE dismisses this with a small, incoherent sound, as if it were an irrelevance. Then she averts her gaze from BRODY, an adieu to him. Only a hand, in a slow, painful convulsion, illustrates her pain. BRODY goes to leave the room, but is stopped by the clatter of the doorbell. He stops briefly, casting a look to his mother. Neither she nor FETCH moves, even if both know the import of the summons. BRODY goes. After a little while, the bell is pulled again. FETCH, the more uncomfortable of the two, seems to concede to it.)

FETCH: I'll go /

(Yet she requires STONE to authorize her. STONE, without haste, relaxes her pose and turns to FETCH, an expression of profound calm on her features. She does not satisfy FETCH with any instruction.)

I'll go /

(Yet she does not. In her frustration she is nearly brutal.)

IT'S THE TELEGRAM /

(STONE does not reply. FETCH shakes a hand wildly in her dilemma.)

STONE: We know what's in the telegram /

(The bell clatters again.)

FETCH: We do / we do know what's in the telegram /

(She lacks an argument.)

But the boy / he / the telegraph boy / he /

(She draws strength from a thought.)

He has many to deliver / I expect /

(She sweeps out. STONE is a picture of patience, but something is unresolved in her. She moves a step or two. She comes to a conclusion.)

STONE: We stand on the dead /

(A cry off, of surprise and ecstasy.)

We /

(She is lucid.)

To be higher / stand on them /

(FETCH'S cry is subsumed in laughter. A powerful murmur of voices precedes the appearance of BRODY, loosely attired in his greatcoat and shoulder bag. His face is drawn from his ordeal. He stands in the door. For a second or two, STONE will not turn. Then she does. He gazes at her.)

BRODY: It's over /

(They are separated by a gulf of pain and longing. STONE'S face and what is written on it, are invisible to the audience.)

*

IMMENSE KISS

Characters

VOXALL   A Young Soldier

IPSA   An Old Woman

CHILD   A Voice

1

An obscurity. Barely discernible, a decayed bed. On it, a sprawling old woman. Her long limbs overhang. The musical rhythms of a ruptured water pipe. Rarely, the flashes, but not the reverberations, of detonations, distantly. The shrill voice of a child, also at intervals, but near.

CHILD: She didn't go /

> *(The pipe alters its insistent rhythm.)*

> she could have / she could have / but she didn't go /

> *(The pipe reverts.)*

> I don't know why she didn't go /

> *(An interval of sound and light.)*

> she could have /

> *(The pipe alters again.)*

> she could have /

2

A male figure enters, idly. He does not regard the bed or the woman. The pipe, the flashes, persist for some time, then falter, and cease.

VOXALL: If I don't go / what does that mean / if I could go / but do not go / that means /

> *(He frowns.)*

> something /

> *(He develops the thought.)*

> it means <u>something</u> not to go when I might go /

> *(He works.)*

it means / it means /

(He articulates.)

whilst I cannot know the consequences of my decision not to go /

(He ponders.)

in choosing not to go I /

CHILD: She could have /

VOXALL: SHE COULD HAVE / BUT SHE DID NOT / SO /

(He smiles oddly.)

she accepts the consequences of <u>not</u> going /

(A thought erupts.)

AND IS IT NOT PROFOUNDLY DISINGENUOUS TO CLAIM YOU DO NOT KNOW THE CHARACTER / THE FORM / THE / THE / THE /

(He shakes his head in his frustration.)

SHAPE /

(And smiles again.)

of these consequences / most disingenuous? / because whilst strictly speaking you cannot <u>know</u> / certainly you might infer / or / if you are incapable of inference / you might imagine / or if you lack imagination /

(He laughs at his inventory.)

you surely must have heard /

(He controls his wit.)

THE RUMOUR /

(He persists.)

and if / out of conceit and arrogance / you disdain the rumour /

(He is triumphant now.)

there is the thing called history / miss /

(He gazes ahead.)

CHILD: I don't know why she didn't go /

(VOXALL is silent, complete.)

IPSA: *(At long last.)* I'm 80 /

(VOXALL seems not to have heard.)

I'm 80 /

(And remains thus.)

80 / I said /

(For the first time, VOXALL turns to face the bed and its occupant.)

VOXALL: I heard you /

(They study one another. The flashes illuminate the room. The ruptured pipe resumes its eccentric rhythms. Their gaze is unbroken. As suddenly as they started, the effects cease.)

3

IPSA: You're in my room /

(VOXALL ignores IPSA'S rebuke.)

VOXALL: The best poets / who are they / those / I think / who / fatigued with the obligation to describe /

(He meditates.)

propose /

(He exclaims.)

but they must be careful / oh / so careful / exhortation in
the mouths of poets / we recoil / we fling the little volume
in the ditch / I've seen it / poems like panicked birds flying
out the turret of a tank / we repudiate your squalid instinct
for coercion /

(He is triumphant.)

LEAVE THAT TO THE IDEOLOGISTS /

(He frowns. He is modest)

I am a poet myself /

(IPSA says nothing.)

no / the proposition / if it is a proposition / must be uttered
oh so / tentatively / or less even / less than uttered /

(He seeks a better word.)

breathed /

(He is satisfied.)

yes / the poet breathes /

(He turns to IPSA.)

the poet breathes / and shallowly / shallow with anxiety /

(He appeals to her.)

never must he say 'do this' / only / 'could this be so?' /

(IPSA gazes unflinchingly at VOXALL.)

IPSA: Poet / you are in my room /

(VOXALL is blasé.)

VOXALL: A filthy room /

(They stare for a long time.)

IPSA: I'm 80 /

(He is piqued by her repetition.)

80 / and you are in my room /

VOXALL: FILTHY / FILTHY IS YOUR ROOM /

(He is surprised at his vehemence. He subdues his temper. The pipe and the flash commence their rhythms.)

4

The effects cease. IPSA and VOXALL sustain an unfaltering gaze.

VOXALL: You could have gone / in which case / having entered your filthy room / I should have left it again / finding nothing to detain me /

(IPSA does not shrink.)

IPSA: And it's me / is it / an old woman of 80 / who detains you? /

(VOXALL is not provoked, but returns to his theme.)

VOXALL: This breathing / this scarcely-audible / and always / always tentative /

IPSA: Don't let me detain you /

VOXALL: So tentative you cannot know for certain if you heard correctly or if /

IPSA: Just go /

VOXALL: It is you yourself who made meaning / this meaning / or that meaning / from words so exquisitely crafted they defy interpretation / no /

(He is certain, satisfied.)

this is the way of the great poet and he is /

(He tosses his head strangely.)

EVEN TO HIMSELF /

(He stares at IPSA.)

INTOLERABLE /

(She is unafraid.)

go where / I am the conqueror / go where / we won / you lost / go where /

(He switches swiftly.)

I am just such a poet /

(He removes his gaze from IPSA, and drifts a few paces.)

and I walk in fear of my own /

IPSA: I don't like poetry /

(He hears, he gnaws a finger, then bursts out laughing.)

CHILD: I don't know why she didn't go / she could have / she could have /

(VOXALL shakes his head wistfully. The pipe, but not the lights, resumes its percussive rhythm, and ceases.)

5

VOXALL: For example /

IPSA: *(Severely.)* Don't /

VOXALL: For example /

IPSA: Don't give me an example /

(They glare in contradiction.)

of the thing you fear to contemplate /

(VOXALL looks, governing his resentment. IPSA removes her gaze from him. She is nervous. She plucks a bed sheet.)

I'm 80 /

(She ventures an opinion.)

and is it fear in any case / you call it fear /

(He studies her.)

80 /

VOXALL: It represents itself as fear /

(She shrugs, as if irritated.)

but much that /

IPSA: Yes /

VOXALL: Whilst unfamiliar /

IPSA: Yes /

(VOXALL is surprised by IPSA'S endorsement, but proceeds.)

VOXALL: Is scarcely /

(He shrugs, choosing a word.)

reprehensible /

(She watches him.)

is fearful at first sight /

IPSA: I'm 80 / and I know everything /

(VOXALL is half-inclined to believe this, yet resents her. He resorts to a threat.)

VOXALL: I AM THE CONQUEROR /

(Surprised by his own vehemence, he laughs. He shakes his head as if to clear it.)

the things we / oh / the miles and the things we /

(He lifts a hand, a gesture of hopelessness.)

poets / desk clerks / well-diggers / the miles / and the things we /

(He abruptly changes the subject.)

AND I THOUGHT THIS / LOOKING BACKWARDS /
THOUGHT / THIS / THIS / ANNIHILATION OF THINGS /
THIS / SCORCHED AND /

(He laughs falsely.)

grass again soon / oh yes / grass and grazing /

(He appeals to IPSA unknowingly.)

the terrible things are also brief /

(He warms to his theme.)

you think / this kiss / this purple evening of whispering
and birdsong / I ache to think how brief it is / it can't be
held / it can't be stopped /

(He shakes his head nostalgically.)

TRUE ALSO OF BARBARITY /

IPSA: *(Who has heard him.)* I'm 80 /

VOXALL: YES / AND YOU KNOW EVERYTHING /

(He looks cruelly at IPSA.)

drag the sheet off yourself /

(The pipe drips in its panicked way. IPSA denies him.)

6

*Piqued by her silent refusal, VOXALL drags his pistol from its holster.
The pipe ceases as abruptly as it started. VOXALL senses absurdity. He
bites his lip.*

CHILD: She didn't go / she could have / but she didn't go /

(VOXALL lets time pass. The gun hangs limply from his fingers.)

VOXALL: Or I will /

(The threat is not vicious. IPSA is contained.)

IPSA: If you are thinking /

CHILD: She didn't / did she /

IPSA: The reason I chose not to go /

CHILD: SHE DID NOT GO /

IPSA: Was in order you / or another like you /

(VOXALL cannot bear to hear her put words to the thing he contemplates.)

VOXALL: No / no /

(He is irritable.)

obviously / no /

IPSA: I am 80 /

VOXALL: You are 80 /

IPSA: To go / what is that / to go? / to go is to continue / I know everything / there is no more to know / and this is my room /

(She gazes at VOXALL, without temper. He plays with his gun. He puts it away.)

VOXALL: You know everything / but me / I don't / and you must be the subject of my education /

(She is apprehensive.)

you and I / we /

(He hesitates.)

why don't <u>you</u> remove the sheet / it's /

(He waves an arm vaguely.)

the decorum of it / vastly better / don't you agree / than me / like some drunk / I've seen it / lout / all fists and / I've seen it / HORRIBLE / I'VE SEEN IT /

(IPSA does not comply.)

and I've only so much time /

IPSA: Listen / like most young men / you are a somewhat pitiful /

VOXALL: Remove the sheet /

IPSA: And somewhat vulgar / half-tottering / half-collapsing / heap / of ill-fitting parts /

VOXALL: *(Resolutely.)* Old woman / I am seeing you /

IPSA: Shift the pieces of your mind around / a little more in this box / a little less in that /

VOXALL: *(Repudiating this.)* I AM A POET /

(She is afraid of him.)

A POET /

(She holds his frantic regard.)

AND POETS / WE ARE / INCHOATE /

(She falters. VOXALL is swiftly calm, retrospective.)

strictly speaking / I don't know when the breath / the breath of the proposition / actually arrived / in the street? / at the foot of the stairs? / I can't be sure / certainly the moment the child said / 'she hasn't gone / she's still there' / I /

(He bites his lip.)

anyway / it's not a breath now / it's a /

(He exults.)

IT YELLS IN MY EARS /

(He is hushed now, almost benign.)

draw away the sheet now / draw it away /

(He looks at the floor.)

darling /

(The word is so shocking to IPSA, she audibly gasps.)

IPSA: You are not /

VOXALL: Yes /

IPSA: *(Indignant.)* You are not seriously /

VOXALL: Yes /

IPSA: Employing that word /

VOXALL: EMPLOYING /

(IPSA shakes her head in her incredulity.)

EMPLOYING THE WORD /

(She observes him.)

you /

(He closes his eyes.)

you do not know everything /

(He takes a few steps towards the bed.)

not <u>employing</u> the word /

(He studies her. He puts out one hand to the edge of the sheet. Her look defies him. He goes to draw it away. Her hand clings to the sheet. The sound of the ruptured pipe. The flashes distantly. She lets go.)

7

IPSA is naked under the sheet. She closes her eyes. VOXALL is statue-still in his contemplation of her body. They remain in this configuration. At long last, IPSA speaks, without opening her eyes.

IPSA: Everything that could be said of me / everything /

(She opens her eyes.)

has been said /

(He does not move his eyes from her.)

strange / how narrow and / derivative / the vocabulary of desire is /

(She is no longer afraid.)

and where desire <u>isn't</u> / not a lot more language / not a lot less /

(Time elapses painfully.)

VOXALL: *(Lifting his gaze to the ceiling.)* When the child said / 'she didn't go / she could have / but she didn't go' / I did not know / I could not know / who this <u>she</u> was / so I /

(He stops his narrative.)

IPSA: Don't lie /

VOXALL: *(Abruptly.)* ASKED /

(He lets this settle.)

and getting the reply / 'the old woman' / heard /

(He nods.)

THAT IS WHEN IT WAS /

(And nods.)

heard my breath / <u>propose</u> /

(His gaze seems fixed on the ceiling.)

IPSA: Listen / I'm frail / and where I'm touched / I bruise /

(He is unmoved.)

you've seen me / now you can go /

(She is rash.)

OR SHOOT ME / SHOOT ME /

VOXALL: Yes /

IPSA: SHOOT /

VOXALL: AND THAT IS SOMETHING YOU DON'T KNOW /

(He laughs oddly.)

and they do / always / this killing of old women /

(At last his head tilts down. He regards her.)

I wonder why / when /

(The sight of IPSA'S nakedness takes his breath away. He puts a hand to his head to steady himself.)

I'll say / about your beauty / I'll say /

(He might, but sways.)

WHOLE BOOKS /

(IPSA gazes.)

IPSA: You are a / such a / brilliant boy / and war / has made more from you than even you / I daresay / anticipated /

(She is perfectly at ease.)

now / cover me / and go /

(They watch.)

my nameless body / and you / nameless /

(He aches.)

namelessly you came / namelessly go /

(VOXALL is not to be manipulated. He seems to ponder her proposal.)

VOXALL: Darling /

IPSA: *(Conceding.)* Darling if you /

VOXALL: Darling /

IPSA: Darling if you wish /

(IPSA smiles, sensing she has an ascendancy over him.)

darling / go /

(To her horror, IPSA observes VOXALL loosen his belt and holster, and hears it fall to the floor. Now he unbuttons his military coat. She resorts to her most severe tone.)

listen /

(He proceeds to his shirt.)

I do not love you /

(She hears herself with a peculiar objectivity, and laughs at the absurd irrelevance of her complaint. Immediately she smothers it.)

DO NOT UNDRESS IN MY ROOM /

(VOXALL hesitates, but briefly. He drags off his shirt.)

listen /

(He holds the shirt loosely in one hand.)

listen /

(IPSA is breathless with anxiety, all confidence fled.)

VOXALL: Darling /

IPSA: Listen /

VOXALL: Darling me /

(She frowns. Her contempt returns in abundance.)

IPSA: Darling <u>you</u>? /

(She recoils from his insolence.)

<u>me</u> / darling <u>you?</u> /

(She shakes her head.)

I am 80 / and weak / and you are /

(She senses the futility of rebuking him.)

let an old woman keep one word / in this filthy world / let her keep one word clean /

(She indicts him.)

POET /

(IPSA glares. VOXALL meditates a long time, then, letting the shirt fall to the floor, goes to the bed and sits at the foot. The flashes begin, illuminating them.)

8

The flashes diminish, then cease.

VOXALL: *(In awe.)* How beautiful your long legs are /

IPSA: *(Defensively.)* Silly /

VOXALL: *(Without menace.)* I am the conqueror / and I say they are /

(IPSA deems it sensible to stay silent.)

and your belly /

(He lifts his eyes to hers.)

and your arse /

IPSA: *(Tentatively.)* But you can't see my arse /

(VOXALL stands and looks down at IPSA, who regrets her remark.)

VOXALL: Exactly so / still / I know the beauty of your arse /

(He feels the compulsion to explain, for himself also.)

'she didn't go' / the child said / at the bottom of the stairs / 'she could have / but she didn't go' /

(He recalls.)

I heard my breath / and with the breath came the decision / not only would I find the room / and enter it / but that you / the tenant of the room / would be / must be / beautiful to me /

(He allows IPSA to absorb the idea.)

IPSA: So /

(She cannot conceal a certain chagrin.)

so / whatever it was / greeted your eyes as you /

(She is provocative.)

STRIPPED ME /

(The words excite VOXALL.)

VOXALL: Darling /

IPSA: However hideous /

VOXALL: Darling /

IPSA: COULD ONLY BE / COULD NOT FAIL TO BE /

(She resents him, profoundly.)

beautiful /

(She rants.)

I AM NOT A WOMAN / I AM AN IDEA TO YOU /

(All the contradictions of her chagrin are evident to both of them. Her lip trembles. VOXALL, by contrast, is coherent.)

VOXALL: Darling / you are an idea / yes / the idea of woman / and me /

(He insists.)

THE IDEA OF MAN /

(He retaliates.)

HALF OF ALL LOVE IS LOVE OF THE IDEA / AND HALF ONLY / IS LOVE /

(He mocks himself.)

did I say half? /

(He smiles.)

I am generous with my half /

(IPSA'S pride abolishes her fear. In a gesture of supreme disdain, she averts her head.)

you love me /

(Appalled, IPSA looks back at him. She shakes her head with a terrible severity. VOXALL is in an agony of desire.)

darling / I must do the act with you / and never mind the darlings / yours or mine /

IPSA: *(Coldly.)* Poet / you cannot do the act <u>with</u> me /

VOXALL: *(Understanding at once.)* No / only <u>to</u> you / it appears /

(He takes one step towards IPSA, who issues a desperate appeal.)

IPSA: IF YOU COME ONTO ME / I'LL BREAK AND BRUISE /

(Her breath comes and goes rapidly.)

I'll break / and bruise /

(VOXALL stares at her pitiful form. The flashes commence.)

CHILD: She could have gone / she could have / but she didn't go /

(The bed is splashed with light.)

preferring to expose herself to circumstances the character of which she could not know /

IPSA: *(Her last throw.)* I'm 80 /

CHILD: Choice /

IPSA: <u>80</u> /

CHILD: A worthless /

IPSA: *(Resorting to any stratagem.)* Darling /

CHILD: Prejudice /

(The ruptured pipe commences.)

it seemed to her /

9

VOXALL, with decision, lifts IPSA into his arms. In the flickering illuminations, he holds her naked body as if it were a treasure retrieved from catastrophe. After some time, the flashes diminish and cease. The pipe becomes silent.

IPSA: I ache /

(VOXALL neither moves nor speaks.)

darling / I ache /

(She suppresses a gasp of pain.)

it's so / oh so /

(Now she emits a sob.)

I ache /

(The pain engulfs her.)

I ACHE /

VOXALL: It's not the most important thing / this aching /

(IPSA winces in her discomfort.)

the bruises /

(She sobs, from fear and pain.)

the dislocation of / or /

IPSA: *(A sudden dread.)* DON'T DROP ME / DARLING /

VOXALL: Fractures to /

IPSA: *(In despair.)* Don't drop me /

(She is childlike.)

don't drop me /

(VOXALL is patient.)

VOXALL: No / the important thing is /

(He seems to assess.)

what I do with what I have stolen /

(IPSA is apprehensive.)

because I've stolen you /

(He laughs.)

AND THEY TAKE VASES / THE SOLDIERS / GROTESQUE ORNAMENTS / PIANOS THEY DON'T KNOW HOW TO PLAY / AND THROW THEM ON THE BACKS OF LORRIES /

(He shakes his head.)

labelled / obviously / 'sergeant Gang / his Persian rug' / 'the clock of Captain Pritkoff' / etcetera / but me /

(He is in thrall to IPSA.)

my exquisite / fragile / barely living / but so living / property /

IPSA: *(In fear and shame.)* Poet / I am pissing over you /

(The CHILD's voice floats in.)

CHILD: She could have gone /

IPSA: *(Humiliated.)* Pissing /

CHILD: She could have /

IPSA: Over you /

(VOXALL holds her in absolute stillness.)

CHILD: She could have /

(VOXALL lifts IPSA higher in his arms, and kisses her mouth.)

but she didn't go /

(VOXALL transports IPSA to the wrecked bed and with infinite tenderness, lays her there.)

VOXALL: No / that is a misapprehension / she could not go /

(He steps back, studies IPSA.)

in this flaming city they abandoned her / a solitary old woman / in order to mock me /

(He imitates their voice.)

'you want tribute? / there's tribute / conqueror' /

(His laugh is strange.)

and the Greeks / Neoptolemus / Menelaus / squabbling in the wreck of Troy /

(He mocks.)

those looted wives / their fluid wombs / their black hair cascading / chased down avenues and howling /

(He mocks again.)

ha / and you are 80 / and to lift a limb hurts you /

(He surges.)

I AM NOT MOCKED /

(He strides to the door to address the invisible CHILD.)

TELL THEM / THIS DECAYED TROPHY IS MY
PREFERENCE /

(He laughs.)

say / say she is vastly / vastly more / and more deeply /
beautiful than any woman in her youth / her prime / her
anything /

(He calls down the staircase.)

DESCRIBE MY ECSTASY /

*(He returns to IPSA, and scrutinizes her. She feels his gaze on her
body.)*

IPSA: *(Moved by him.)* You know /

VOXALL: I do know / yes /

IPSA: Whatever the facts /

VOXALL: *(They are in profound accord.)* Yes /

IPSA: The pains / the piss / the way the flesh / as if ashamed /

VOXALL: Shame on its shame /

IPSA: Slips off my bones /

   (They adore.)

VOXALL: Pity the facts / the lonely <u>facts</u> / the facts which /
oh / would so like to be synonymous with <u>truth</u> / but
which can never be /

   (He smiles.)

the lonely facts /

(They share an exquisite regard.)

IPSA: Your scrutiny / your terrible scrutiny of me /

(He looks, and looks.)

darling / nameless darling / fetch the gun /

VOXALL: Gun /

IPSA: It's on the floor / your gun /

(He frowns. Suspicion overwhelms him.)

I'm 80 / 80 / 80 / darling / after you / nothing more /

(He tightens his mouth.)

you may not leave me with this <u>nothing</u> <u>more</u> /

(She interprets his confusion.)

I have been four times married / nameless darling / be assured we knew nothing of this / this /

(VOXALL senses he is being brilliantly manipulated, and averts his face, as if it pained him. IPSA ceases. VOXALL starts to utter, stops, begins again.)

VOXALL: Always / always / in love / this dread / this dread /

IPSA: *(Cutting in.)* Yes /

VOXALL: This dread you are not / either of you / honest / that you think this / and she /

(His shrug is melancholy.)

she is not thinking it /

IPSA: Yes / and you cannot know /

(His look is pitiful.)

YOU CANNOT KNOW /

(They are at their most intimate. The look between them is a search.)

now / shoot /

(The look lingers on.)

shoot /

VOXALL: *(Shaking off the look.)* STOP SAYING SHOOT / I'LL
SHOOT WHEN I WANT TO / IF I WANT TO / I WILL SHOOT /

(He is ashamed of his temper.)

you make me infantile /

*(As if to confirm it, he stamps his foot on the floor. IPSA is able to
smile.)*

IPSA: Say / when you meet your comrades / drunk and jeering
round a fire of wardrobes / crucifixes / picture frames /
say / 'I found an old woman in an upstairs room / and
infuriated that she was not young / I' /

(She lifts a hand in a gesture of futility.)

if / as you say / they always kill old women / they'll think /
'the poet's just like us' /

(IPSA smiles.)

scarcely an atrocity / shooting me / and a small price to
pay for their affection / love / loyalty / whatever soldiers
share / and which you might need one day /

(She creates the word anew.)

darling /

*(VOXALL is bewildered, his feelings in chaos. He strides one way,
and at once returns. He holds a finger aloft.)*

VOXALL: This / this / all this /

(He seethes.)

AND I STARTED IT /

(His mouth is tight.)

this / argument / elaboration /

(He shudders.)

DESIRE / IT ABHORS DEBATE /

(IPSA watches him, bemused.)

I can neither fuck nor kill /

(He glares at IPSA in his exasperation.)

CHILD: She could have gone /

VOXALL: *(Brutally.)* SHUT UP /

CHILD: I don't know why she didn't go /

VOXALL: *(Bawling.)* I WILL MURDER YOU /

(The CHILD is silenced. VOXALL sways in his delirium.)

I am leaving this room / I am putting on my coat /

(He sweeps his greatcoat off the floor, and flings it on.)

and leaving this room / at the bottom of the stairs I am turning around / and coming up again / and I will enter here with neither poetry / nor pity /

(IPSA does not appear intimidated. VOXALL goes to march out.)

IPSA: Gun /

(He stops. His face is awful.)

VOXALL: And God help you /

(He stares witheringly. He seizes the holster belt and leaves. IPSA strains to hear, then, with an effort, climbs off the bed, and wrapping herself in the sheet, goes to the door. She has hardly lifted a hand to steady herself when a shot reverberates from below. The slightest movement of her head reveals her shock, her incredulity. The rhythm of the ruptured pipe begins. VOXALL enters, and ignoring IPSA, goes to the bed and flings himself on it.)

10

Both are still. VOXALL studies her. At last IPSA must cry out.

IPSA: *(Calling down.)* CHILD /

> *(She suffers the silence. Now her voice echoes down the stairs.)*
>
> CHILD /
>
> *(There is no reply. The pipe falters, stops. IPSA turns to face VOXALL.)*
>
> you did not shoot the child /
>
> *(She is confident of her own interpretation of events.)*
>
> you sent the child away /
>
> *(VOXALL'S face is lifeless.)*
>
> and fired into the floor /
>
> *(She laughs, mildly.)*
>
> to impress me with your violence / to show / oh / whatever a poet needs to show when a woman claims to <u>know</u> him /
>
> *(She is complacent.)*
>
> you fired into the floor /
>
> *(VOXALL reveals nothing.)*
>
> 'go' / you said / 'here's fifty cents / buy an ice-cream' /
>
> *(She immediately corrects herself.)*
>
> not an ice-cream / in the middle of a war / silly / no /
>
> *(She smiles at herself.)*
>
> you raised a fist to her / no need to land the blow / she fled /
>
> *(He is cold.)*
>
> AND YOU FIRED INTO THE FLOOR /

(Her hope hangs in the air.)

give me my bed /

(VOXALL denies her.)

my knees / my hips / oh / give me my bed /

(His immobility is his reply. IPSA shakes her head, the vaguest smile on her lips.)

the poet acts the sadist /

(Her mockery is mild.)

not very convincingly /

(She risks.)

oh / little / little / wolf / I am 80 / and you cannot /

VOXALL: *(Simply.)* She's dead /

IPSA: MAKE ME DREAD YOU /

VOXALL: The child /

(IPSA disbelieves him, more from an act of will than any conviction.)

something / something I could not define / something I could not identify / was absent from our last encounter /

(He is thoughtful.)

IPSA: *(In pain.)* Can't stand /

VOXALL: So much was extraordinary / unique perhaps / and yet /

IPSA: CAN'T STAND ANY LONGER /

VOXALL: *(Ignoring her pain.)* There was a lack /

(He works at the thought.)

so significant this lack / you may yourself have felt it /

(He looks at her.)

sacrifice /

(He is glad to possess the word.)

<u>sacrifice</u> was the lack /

(IPSA is profoundly apprehensive.)

at the foot of the stairs / and only there / among the
broken glass / and spent bullets / the very place where it /
we / our /

(He bites his lip.)

where this began /

(He smiles forlornly.)

did it become glaringly obvious to me /

(He is confirmed.)

AND SHE WAS THERE / SHE / AS IT WERE /

(He frowns in his amazement.)

proposed herself /

*(IPSA forgets the pain in her joints, certain the CHILD is dead.
VOXALL'S expression confirms it for her.)*

I am certain / had you been young / a wife / an
adolescent / and therefore / how shall I say / the
<u>predictable</u> <u>subjects</u> <u>of</u> <u>violation</u> / such sacrifice would not
have seemed appropriate / or even necessary /

(IPSA is near to fainting. But she is desperate, arbitrary.)

IPSA: YOU FIRED INTO THE FLOOR /

(VOXALL'S eyes are lifeless.)

ALL RIGHT / NOT THE FLOOR / THE CEILING /

(His expression is unaltered. IPSA'S horror becomes self-hatred.)

break my bones / and tear me / as if / like an insane
criminal / you ripped open a sack with filthy fingers / and
found it to be / oh yes / as I am /

(She glares at VOXALL.)

AS I AM / EMPTY / AND MADE A FIRE OF IT IN HIS
MADNESS / BURN ME /

(She sags.)

burn me /

*(VOXALL is profoundly disappointed, and seems to lack a reply.
Instead, he places his fingers together, and his hands to his lips, a
picture of thoughtfulness.)*

VOXALL: You say / over and over again / 'I am 80' /

(His look is critical.)

why then / must you think the thoughts of a 30 year-old /
an adolescent / even? /

(IPSA is caught by the thought.)

you lay in this bed / and the years ran over you like
animals / and all you thought / if you thought / had been
thought already /

*(Her look is, for the first time, one of self-doubt. VOXALL flings off
the bed with a surge of energy.)*

you have done nothing / since I first entered this room /
this filthy room / but try to divert me from my intention /

(IPSA nods her head.)

to separate my will from my desire /

(And again.)

to weaken / and diminish me /

(And again.)

and always by this pitiful stratagem of claiming some moral ascendancy based entirely / and spuriously / on your 80 years /

(He mocks her.)

'I know everything' /

(IPSA shakes her head as if to rid herself of her presumption.)

IPSA: I know nothing / nothing do I know /

VOXALL: I invite you /

(He holds the idea in his hand.)

I <u>encourage</u> you /

(He shakes his head.)

I INSIST YOU BECOME THIS 80 /

(He is supremely certain.)

Accept my desire / accept my reverence / and do not demean this child's sacrifice /

(IPSA is strangely calm.)

IPSA: You did not fire into the floor /

VOXALL: Not the floor / nor the ceiling / either /

(The knowledge settles in IPSA. She extends a hand. VOXALL goes to her, and assists her to the bed. She stands beside it. Her head turns to look at him. The distant flashes flicker over them. IPSA'S shoulders rise in a great single sob.)

yes /

(She fills her lungs.)

yes /

(He is close to her shoulder and kisses it tenderly.)

how hard it is / to <u>be</u> your age /

IPSA: *(Surprised by her own tears.)* It is years / oh / years / since I wept /

VOXALL: Yes / and I am under no illusion that it is love of me that brings tears to your eyes /

(He looks deeply into her.)

you are taking leave of yourself /

(He is moved.)

a painful parting /

(He draws her face to his, and kisses her profoundly. IPSA is unresisting, but nor does she participate. At last his kiss ends. The flashes cease.)

IPSA: *(With a dread.)* If she /

VOXALL: She won't /

IPSA: The child /

VOXALL: She won't /

IPSA: Came through the door /

VOXALL: She won't come through the door /

IPSA: Or called us / from the foot of the stairs /

(VOXALL does not need to assure her again. IPSA takes a few seconds to complete her thought.)

you'd /

(She finds the word.)

forfeit /

(She assents to her own word.)

forfeit /

VOXALL: *(In complete accord.)* Yes /

IPSA: Every /

VOXALL: Yes /

IPSA: Last fragment of authority you have assumed / and /

VOXALL: Yes / yes /

IPSA: Render yourself /

VOXALL: RIDICULOUS /

(IPSA, knowing the whole of it, is placid. She assents, and the word is a gift, immense, as VOXALL knows.)

IPSA: Yes /

(She gazes into VOXALL.)

a woman /

(She is supremely certain.)

becoming 80 /

(And not unkind.)

becomes stone /

(VOXALL does not contest this.)

all she hears / she hears through stone /

(VOXALL is moved by her.)

and lying under you / stays stone /

(IPSA is not cruel, and VOXALL accepts her challenge.)

VOXALL: I enter stone /

(They are a state of perfect equilibrium. The lights flash, and cease.)

*

CRITIQUE OF PURE FEELING

Characters

MAISNON   A Woman with Land

SED   A Suitor

VAGRANT   Male

1

An old woman on two sticks. She surveys her estate.

MAISNON: I think of land /

    (She gazes a while.)

    there was a time I thought of love /

    (She smiles wanly.)

    what do I mean by land / what did I mean by love /

    (She iterates.)

    'I must own' /

    (And waits.)

    'I must be owned' /

    (She recalls.)

    he travelled me / he measured with his mouth /

    (She phrases meticulously.)

    my whole extent /

    (She laughs mildly.)

    I wasn't used to it / I wasn't / I was so /

    (She stops. She is nostalgic.)

    unused to it /

    (She looks into the distance.)

    one thousand and seven hundred acres / with grazing rights /

    (She reiterates.)

    grazing rights /

(She is bemused.)

over seven hundred more /

(She plays with the word.)

<u>acres</u> /

(And again.)

<u>acres</u> /

(She is nostalgic.)

'your acres' / he said / 'your <u>acres</u> <u>of</u> <u>arse</u>' /

(She frowns.)

I was offended / I wasn't used to it /

(And mildly laughs.)

this saying / this saying of things /

(She is melancholy.)

'I laud you' / he said / 'I laud you' /

(And bites her lip.)

'laud' / I said / '<u>laud?</u>' /

(The memory hurts her.)

he walked away /

(She shakes her head. The regret seems fresh.)

I wasn't used to it /

(She presents the word again.)

<u>lauding</u> /

(She seems to dream. A male figure enters. He scarcely regards her but gazes over the land. For a while both are silent.)

it's mine /

(He ignores her.)

the land /

(He gives nothing.)

I own it /

(He reflects. He does not regard her.)

SED: And your body / whose is that? /

(MAISNON is intimidated, but will not show it.)

MAISNON: You're clever /

SED: Clever / and I like old women /

(Still his gaze is on the horizon.)

not all old women / but what I like in some old women is probably common to them all / it's /

(He hesitates.)

I think about these things /

(He is resigned.)

these unfathomable things /

(Time passes, until the tension compels MAISNON to utter.)

MAISNON: Being clever / it's /

(He is motionless.)

I'm clever / but it doesn't make you happy /

(The proposition is of no interest to SED. She goes on.)

I find /

(And on.)

whereas /

SED: *(A cry.)* Whereas /

(MAISNON is undeterred.)

MAISNON: Land does /

SED: *(Affirming this.)* Mmm / mmm /

    (He nods his head.)

    mmm /

    (His smile is peculiar.)

    and yet /

    (MAISNON cannot resist parodying his manner.)

MAISNON: And yet /

    (SED is provoked and at last turns his gaze to her.)

SED: We're clever / both of us /

    (He is lucid.)

    and if you're not already owned / I'll own you /

    (MAISNON is apprehensive. SED contemplates her.)

    obviously / it comes with obligations /

    (He studies her.)

    these obligations / some onerous perhaps / I will fulfil whilst / at the same time / resenting the restrictions on my freedom that obligation necessarily implies /

    (He chews.)

    still I /

    (And frowns.)

    still I /

    (He finds the words.)

    require the obligations /

(And smiles, as if relieved.)

I think about these things /

(He is resigned.)

these unfathomable things /

(Their mutual regard is sustained. MAISNON has formed an opinion of SED.)

MAISNON: You're passionate / spontaneous / and unpredictable / Mr /

(He seems unwilling to disclose his name. MAISNON persists.)

Mr /

SED: Sed /

MAISNON: Mr /

(She scarcely comprehends his name.)

Sed /

(He watches her intently.)

women fall in love with you / I shouldn't be surprised /

(He does not dissent from this.)

but me / I'm 80 / on two sticks / and I ceased long ago to /

SED: *(Looking away abruptly.)* This /

MAISNON: Contemplate / let alone to /

SED: This /

MAISNON: Participate / in some /

SED: This / this /

(He heaves and shudders. MAISNON is apprehensive and silent. SED recovers.)

over-rehearsed and dismal litany of prevarications and excuses / I will carry you upstairs /

(Still he does not look at her. MAISNON senses the extent of his threat.)

darling /

(He lifts his eyes to her. MAISNON is dry-mouthed.)

MAISNON: Sed /

(She affects bemusement.)

that's unusual /

(He gives nothing.)

Sed / a most unusual name / how is Sed spelled? /

(He waits.)

SED: As in sed / ucer /

(She utters a small sound of amusement, scarcely sincere.)

but I'm not /

MAISNON: No /

SED: Not at all a seducer /

MAISNON: No / I can tell you're not /

(Still he studies her.)

the reason I like land /

(She hesitates, then commits.)

and <u>prefer</u> land / prefer land to people / is this / it's /

SED: Darling / it's all right /

(His tone is assuring, and a surprise to MAISNON.)

I'm kind /

(She is dubious.)

and have land myself /

MAISNON: *(Tentatively.)* So /

   (He waits.)

   so /

   (She is desperate to extricate herself. SED is unexpectedly charming.)

SED: Darling / let me assure you / when I fell in love with you it was not because / seeing you walked with sticks / I knew you could not run away from me /

   (He laughs lightly.)

   how is <u>your</u> name spelled /

   (She gives nothing.)

   or spoken? /

   (She resolves on a stratagem.)

MAISNON: I'm going in now / my husband is expecting me /

SED: *(Ignoring this.)* It looks like mansion on the page / but it is not mansion / is it / it's /

   (He articulates it carefully.)

   <u>mais</u> / <u>non</u> /

   (She does not confirm this.)

   this / I imagine / creates confusion in the simple minds of grocers / tradesmen / and the like / who have heard of <u>mansion</u> and even possibly / from their schooldays / <u>maison</u> / the first word we are taught in French / but /

MAISNON: I'm going in / I said /

SED: Mais non /

   (He ceases, and smiles.)

   confirm for me / please / I utter your name correctly /

(She looks at SED, then goes to leave.)

you have no husband / Maisnon / and the dog you had
has died /

*(She stops, and seems to contemplate her predicament. He waits for
the acquiescence he has all along predicted.)*

MAISNON: I can't be lifted /

(SED nods gravely.)

and I can't lie on my back /

*(He nods again, with a barely-disguised curiosity. She casts an angry
glance at him, and ridicules his proposition.)*

<u>fell</u> in <u>love</u> with <u>me</u> /

*(SED does not defend himself. The old woman sets off. He watches
her depart, his fascination with her evident from the intensity of his
gaze. At last he turns away and walks in the opposite direction.)*

2

MAISNON, wearing an old coat and hat, enters. She gazes out.

MAISNON: It's there / land / always / always there /

(She waits.)

and love's not / not there when you /

*(She abruptly ceases as SED appears, similarly clad for winter. His
manner is cool as before, but his gaze is fixed on her. MAISNON is
shocked but conceals it. At last she speaks.)*

I got to the house / I thought he's following me /

(She waits.)

quietly / quietly following /

(She chooses to be bold with him.)

I wasn't sorry / not in the least sorry / to find that you were not / for one thing /

SED: This /

MAISNON: I was not washed /

SED: This / this /

MAISNON: Not thoroughly / thoroughly washed /

SED: Melancholy recitation of /

MAISNON: The following day / however /

SED: Domestic and hygienic /

MAISNON: I was /

(He is silenced. MAISNON takes her time.)

and all the days of June /

(She plays.)

<u>thoroughly</u> washed /

(She waits.)

but where were you? /

(He is silent, bemused.)

come July I was much less /

(She is unashamed.)

fastidious /

(And waits.)

my hips / my knees /

(They are studying one another.)

etcetera / and you might have been in /

(She is arbitrary.)

<u>Uruguay</u> /

(And without bitterness.)

seducing /

(He looks blandly.)

except you don't /

(SED declines to contribute.)

in August / no / not August / early September / I required a medical examination / this I put off /

(She is unconcealed.)

and off /

(She does not accuse him.)

and I required it / still I put it off / thinking / 'the very day I fail to appear / <u>he</u> will' /

(She bites her lip.)

the pain went /

(She half-laughs.)

or took up residence in another joint /

(She removes her eyes from him and gazes out.)

SED: It's as if /

(He does not complete this thought for some time.)

the sheer immensity of the obligations enhanced the so-brief moment /

(And again.)

during which the obligations were abolished /

(And again.)

in the euphoric oblivion of /

(He sniffs, frowns.)

the act /

(He waits. She stares out.)

and how much greater are these obligations in your case /

(He shakes his head in wonder.)

your hips are worse / if anything / much worse /

(He looks at the ground.)

but are they bad enough? /

(SED surprises MAISNON with this speculation. She turns to look at him.)

I think about these things / these unfathomable things /

(She is wary. SED cheerful.)

who puts you to bed? /

MAISNON: I don't go to bed /

SED: You have a bed / but you don't go there? /

MAISNON: I sleep in a chair /

SED: *(Irritated with himself.)* You said / you said / you said you cannot be horizontal /

(He makes a fist of his hand, a sign of his impatience with himself.)

you said /

(Suddenly he smiles.)

I was confusing you with a woman in Ecuador /

MAISNON: *(Charmed.)* Uruguay /

(SED nods, corrected. He looks at the ground. Time passes.)

SED: Still / there is a bed /

MAISNON: There is a bed /

(SED ponders.)

SED: Somehow / this ownership / with all its onerous /
and possibly suffocating / obligations / demands that
unrelieved proximity implied by / and demonstrated
through / the sharing of the bed /

(She says nothing.)

but you sleep in a chair /

(SED is frustrated.)

we cannot both sleep in this chair / I daresay /

(His look is irritated.)

what are the dimensions of the chair? /

(MAISNON is disenchanted and begins to move off.)

how big's the chair / I said /

*(MAISNON stops. She is afraid of SED, who discovers a reasonable
tone.)*

I am asking things /

(He bites his lip.)

defining and refining things /

(He struggles.)

things /

(And looks at her.)

relevant to marriage /

*(MAISNON understands the gravity of her situation, but not her own
attitude to it. She pokes the ground with one of her sticks. She makes
small sounds of doubt and pleasure. SED attends. At last MAISNON
lifts her gaze to him.)*

MAISNON: Call me darling /

(He waits.)

call me darling again /

(SED senses he is tested. He shapes the word.)

SED: Darling /

(MAISNON assesses his articulation. She frowns. Her regret is tangible.)

MAISNON: It's not the same /

(Her smile is uncomfortable. SED tries humour. He shrugs and smiles.)

SED: Ecuador /

(She refuses this plea and simply studies him.)

it's six months /

(Her look is unaltered.)

more than six months since /

MAISNON: *(Cutting him off.)* Uruguay /

(He is wounded.)

Uruguay / not Ecuador /

(He nods gravely.)

SED: May I /

(She shakes her head. They are poised in opposition.)

Allow me / please / to try another /

(She shakes it more violently.)

a different darling / please /

(By way of reply, MAISNON turns to go.)

it's six months since I said it / six months since you heard it /

(His despair stops her.)

<u>six</u> /

(He cries out.)

<u>six</u> /

(He complains.)

how can you know my /

(MAISNON has ascendancy. She leans on her two sticks.)

from <u>two</u> <u>syllables</u> / how can you know my /

(She sets off. He is desperate.)

<u>darling</u> /

(This may not be the word as previously enunciated, but it charms by its pathos. MAISNON stops, her back to SED. At last she utters.)

MAISNON: These things / these unfathomable things / you think about /

(She warns.)

I never do /

(She waits for his response, which is conciliatory.)

SED: Wise / surely / surely wise /

(His smile is nervous.)

it's not as if this thinking alters in the least my desire or my capacity to /

MAISNON: I'm land / Mr Sed /

(SED is puzzled.)

the way land is /

(He frowns. MAISNON is irritated by his slow uptake.)

I am /

(He is hesitant.)

do you think / walking to the shop /

(She articulates deliberately.)

I'm <u>treading</u> land /

SED: *(Bemused.)* No /

MAISNON: Or seeing swans swim / think / they are on water whereas I / I live on land /

SED: I don't think that / no /

MAISNON: Land's simply /

SED: Land /

(She turns to look at SED, and gazes at him.)

MAISNON: So is my body /

(SED nods seriously.)

and the acts pertaining thereto /

(SED smiles oddly.)

<u>land</u> /

(And nods in accord.)

SED: That's good / that's very good /

(He continues to nod.)

what you describe / in its lack of / or refusal of / awareness / its /

(He smiles to find the word.)

sheer <u>minerality</u> /

(And announces his pleasure.)

perfectly accommodates to my /

(Again he finds the words.)

inextinguishable self-consciousness /

(He is triumphant.)

<u>be</u> land /

(He is without guile.)

<u>darling</u> /

(Whereas MAISNON is dubious again.)

this time <u>I</u> will go towards the house / the house I already call <u>our</u> <u>home</u> / and you will follow / seeing / this time / that I don't <u>deviate</u> /

(He laughs lightly.)

and end up in /

(He thinks briefly.)

<u>Uruguay</u> /

(He passes her, to set off in the direction of the house. MAISNON does not move.)

MAISNON: Laud me /

(SED stops.)

SED: *(Charmed.)* Laud you? /

MAISNON: Laud me / yes / before we go /

(SED'S pleasure dissipates. He is swiftly grave.)

SED: Mineral needs to know /

MAISNON: Yes /

SED: Its gravity is undiminished /

(She waits. He studies her.)

80 / so what /

MAISNON: So what /

SED: Its mass draws / its bulk exerts /

(They are poised in tension. He lauds her.)

it pulls / it is the law /

(MAISNON thrills.)

MAISNON: Laud /

(She demands.)

laud /

SED: I am / I am lauding /

MAISNON: Laud / more /

(SED contemplates her.)

SED: I'm going in /

MAISNON: Laud /

SED: And you / you follow / follow on your sticks /

MAISNON: Laud /

(SED detects her fear of him.)

SED: You will find me there / naked and waiting /

(MAISNON is silent now.)

go to the chair that serves you for a bed / where I will lever you / as great rocks are levered out of earth /

(Her listening is agony.)

levered and upturned /

(He is studied in his speech.)

343

and seeing you I'll say /

(They are in thrall.)

'these acres / these pale acres of your arse' /

(He ceases. She heeds his lauding.)

MAISNON: Go then /

(He waits.)

go /

(Without a look, SED walks away, towards the house. MAISNON is dead still for a time, then turns. She watches his departure. Suddenly she flings away one of her sticks, then with determination, the other. For a while she hangs on the air, then sinks to the ground with a small cry. Dusk descends on her.)

3

An irritable, plucking wind runs over the land. MAISNON'S clothing is flicked, flattens, and is flicked again. A VAGRANT insinuates himself into the scene. It is not SED. The VAGRANT observes MAISNON, or her corpse, he is unsure which. A distant sound of the last train. The VAGRANT comes nearer and is about to kneel alongside MAISNON when she speaks.

MAISNON: It's mine /

(The VAGRANT stops in mid-move.)

the land /

(After a moment's reflection, the VAGRANT, not without a certain tenderness, extends himself over her. The wind. The dark. At last light creeps in with dawn. The VAGRANT climbs off MAISNON and going a few feet from her, pisses. The first train of the day, distantly. Some sense he is being watched causes the VAGRANT to look, without concern, to SED, who has entered and stands. The VAGRANT adjusts his clothing and walks off. MAISNON is dead still, as all along.)

SED: A killer /

(She is silent.)

that /

(He is irritable.)

that / that /

(She is silent.)

a killer /

(He sways on his feet.)

the armchair / very comfortable / I thought / 'she's on her way' / naked on the armchair / 'slow / obviously /

(He squirms.)

but on her way' /

(He bites his lip anxiously.)

two clocks chimed /

(He laughs falsely.)

delay / I love delay / but /

(MAISNON slowly comes onto one elbow. She peers dimly over the land.)

sexual love without delay /

(He clears his throat.)

for idiots / but /

(They are silent for a time.)

I thought / 'she's had a fall' /

(He laughs briefly.)

I love that phrase / 'had a fall' / not 'fell over' / '<u>had</u> <u>a</u> <u>fall</u>' /

(He is pensive.)

in her haste to be <u>upturned</u> by me /

(He chooses his words.)

she's <u>gone</u> <u>down</u> <u>and</u> <u>smashed</u> <u>a</u> <u>hip</u> /

(He gazes over the land now.)

this posed a problem for me /

(He muses.)

an immense problem / because /

(His hesitation is brief.)

allow me to articulate the problem /

(She says nothing.)

whilst your crippled condition / your age / your two sticks / your awkwardness and frailty / were the origins of the desire I felt for you /

(He strains to communicate with MAISNON.)

the so / so / delicate relation between your sexual power and your incapacity /

(He knots his hands.)

I think of these things / these unfathomable things /

(She lends him nothing.)

critically depends upon /

(He is suddenly simple.)

your sickness being not greater than your appetite for love /

(MAISNON says nothing for a long time. Then she attempts to climb to her feet. SED does not assist her, knowing she would refuse him. She achieves her aim.)

MAISNON: I have a shotgun /

SED: I saw it / leaning up against the kitchen wall /

(She is silent, watching him. He predicts her threat.)

and if you had it /

(He laughs, naturally and beautifully.)

silly /

MAISNON: Yes /

SED: Silly because /

MAISNON: Yes /

SED: I was only being /

(He stops.)

ha /

(He bites his lip.)

I say <u>only</u> /

(His smile remains.)

<u>only</u> being frank with you /

(They study one another. He goes to fetch her dropped sticks, one after the other.)

MAISNON: The killer kept me warm /

SED: Yes / and it was a bitter / bitter night / I gave up being naked rather sooner than I expected to /

MAISNON: I said / 'it's mine / the land' /

SED: As you are inclined to do /

MAISNON: As I am inclined to / but he just /

SED: Yes / the killer is a trespasser /

(His casual manner ceases.)

I didn't hear you shout /

(Again they are opposed. MAISNON waits.)

MAISNON: I didn't /

SED: You fell / but /

MAISNON: Sank /

(He frowns.)

SED: You did not fall /

MAISNON: Sank to my knees /

(SED must examine this. He walks in a circle, stops, shrugs.)

SED: So /

(Now he understands nothing.)

so /

(She will not enlighten him.)

filled with anxiety and /

(He is not convinced of this.)

weak with anticipation of our beautiful encounter / my nakedness and yours so soon to be /

(He commits to it nevertheless.)

how might you have seen this killer / this trespasser and killer / stealthily advancing when /

(He affects to smile.)

your neck will not turn even forty-five degrees /

(MAISNON watches.)

MAISNON: I sank before that /

(SED bites his lip.)

SED: Before that? / you sank before he /

MAISNON: Long before he / yes /

(He waits, hiding his impatience.)

lying there / I heard the foxes / after the foxes / the midnight train /

SED: *(As if relieved.)* I heard the midnight train /

(He smiles.)

curled up in the armchair / no longer naked / and thinking surely she keeps a rug somewhere /

(He affects to laugh.)

I heard the midnight train /

(MAISNON is not forthcoming.)

so /

(He must know.)

the killer / the killer and the trespasser / did not cause your /

(He likes the word.)

sinking? /

(She watches, but her body aches.)

but simply / trespassing / he /

MAISNON: I'm cold /

SED: Cold / yes / cold without the trespasser /

(MAISNON does not reply to this, but stiffly makes to go home. Her body is reluctant. She emits a stifled groan, and steadies herself. SED watches, immobile. She tries again, and fails again.)

lying out all night /

(He shrugs.)

at 80 /

(He stares at MAISNON.)

even with a killer as a rug /

(He shrugs again. He is overswept by incredulity and temper.)

sinking / sinking as you did /

(A thought intervenes.)

onto your own land / your own land admittedly /

(He is in pieces.)

did you not think /

(He shakes his head.)

think / no / why think / thinking / irrelevant /

(He reposes the question.)

what caused you to suffocate the instinct / to cry out to me? /

(MANSION looks at the ground.)

the dew / the damp / the murderer / all converging on you /

(Not replying to him, MAISNON knows he must deduce the reason, which he does.)

you dreaded me /

(He frowns deeper than ever before.)

dreaded me /

(The word is odd now in his mouth.)

darling /

(She does not dissent.)

dreaded me / and preferred to die /

(He gasps. He is cruel.)

on your own land / obviously / and certain / from your little knowledge of me / I would not come looking for you with a torch /

(Still she will not look at SED, who speculates further.)

but then / oh /

(He shakes his head, and a deep laugh rises in him.)

a murderer interrupts the suicide /

(He throws back his head. The laugh is not contrived.)

a perfect coalescence / surely / but /

(He recovers.)

he does not kill / and she does not die /

(The facts of the case put an end to his humour.)

fascinating but you're cold / and I /

(He hesitates.)

in Ecuador perhaps / might find / and laud / some old woman more inclined to /

(Speaking this frivolity produces a confusion in SED'S thought. Now they look into each other with a profundity that had not existed hitherto.)

to /

(He suffers this dread.)

to /

(He becomes enraged.)

inclined to what / to what / to what /

(He strips off his jacket.)

put this on / put this on / you'll catch your /

(He advances towards her.)

MAISNON: *(Defiantly.)* No /

SED: *(Trying to drape her.)* You will / you will / you'll catch your /

(She averts her face. SED ceases to argue.)

it's nothing to me whether you catch your death or not /

MAISNON: *(Uncritically.)* It isn't / is it? /

SED: *(Sipping on the jacket.)* No / it's not / I was /

(He stops.)

I was /

(He reflects.)

plucking pity off the floor / and in its banal obligations / trying to obliterate the question I had asked myself / the question which /

(He smiles feebly.)

here / or in Ecuador / can't be asked / because it can't be answered /

(He is enraged.)

but I'm clever / clever / clever and I ask /

(He reiterates.)

'inclined to what?' /

(Now he mocks himself.)

'I think about these things /

(And mocks more deeply.)

these unfathomable things' /

(Time passes. MAISNON is entirely aware, as never before, of her own and his agony.)

MAISNON: And I thought / washing thoroughly / thoroughly washed / he could so easily / with his /

(She smiles.)

capacity for <u>lauding</u> / and his looks / have younger women / women without sticks / who /

(Her smile becomes ironic.)

lifted and laid on their backs /

(She laughs with contempt.)

could not / for a single hour even of his day / abolish the pain of Mr Sed /

(Her gaze on him is kind now.)

for him / sticks are necessary / and I / silly misapprehension / need never wash / let alone thoroughly /

(She erupts in a certainty more profound than his own.)

you are not more horrified than me by /

(She cannot discover the word she might prefer.)

<u>the</u> <u>fuck</u> /

(Her face is pained. She forces herself.)

<u>the</u> <u>fact</u> <u>of</u> <u>the</u> <u>fuck</u> /

(She shakes her head so slowly.)

that word / that word indicts itself / and you won't hear it said again by me /

(She looks at the ground. SED is moved.)

SED: You are not land /

(She barely affirms his judgement. He is hesitant in going to her, as if a rule had changed. She takes his arm. They make a move towards the house.)

did he /

(They stop.)

the trespasser / the murderer / the <u>rug</u> / did he /

(He cannot pose the question fully.)

did he /

(MAISNON cannot or will not reply to this, which is no surprise to SED. They advance a further painful step. SED is cheerful.)

this is a subject which / inevitably / will /

(She lets out a stifled cry and stops. SED is patient.)

on those long evenings of anger and /

(Again her hip hurts and she utters a cry.)

beauty / which extend before us /

(He is patient as an animal, supporting her. When she is ready she moves again.)

darling /

(She is so cautious in her movement and stops. SED attends. At last she moves. SED is crucified by his own meditation.)

did he / darling / did he /

(She grits her teeth and moves.)

did he /

(They edge off. Now he cries out bitterly.)

<u>did</u> he /

(They are out of sight. He laughs at his own rancour. He speaks more benignly.)

did he / though /

(Now the laughter of them both can be heard, sweetly as a stream.)

*

WWW.OBERONBOOKS.COM

www.ingramcontent.com/pod-product-compliance
Ingram Content Group UK Ltd.
Pitfield, Milton Keynes, MK11 3LW, UK
UKHW020720280225
455688UK00012B/440